Freedom through knowledge

EDUCATION, TRAINING AND SUSTAINABILITY

Conditions for success in a changing world

The following persons collaborated on the publication of this book:
Gil Rémillard, *Publisher*
Marie-Christine DuPont, *Editor in Chief*
Martin Dumas, *Coordinator*
Martin Dumas and Rochelle Lash, *Research and editing*

Distribution: Messageries ADP
Edition Management: Decision Media
Translation: Nicolas Godin, Marie-Michèle Lapointe-Cloutier, Françoise Miquet,
    Mary-Rose Morrison, Daniel Saykaly
Revision and Proofreading: Louise Letendre, Françoise Miquet, Daniel McBride and Mary-
    Rose Morrison
Cover page graphic design: Philippe O'Connor
Typesetting: Guy Verville
Printing: LithoChic
Cover page images: Robert Kohlhuber, Viorika Prikhodko

Legal Deposit: 4th quarter 2008
Bibliothèque et Archives nationales du Québec
Library and Archives Canada

ISBN : 978-2-9808532-7-2
Printed in Canada

Decision Media
2075 University Street, Suite 1217
Montreal, Quebec
H3A 2L1

Phone: 514 871-2225
Fax: 514 871-2226
www.conferenceofmontreal.com

This book has been published in collaboration
with the International Economic Forum of the
Americas/Conference of Montreal

THE
INTERNATIONAL
ECONOMIC FORUM
OF THE AMERICAS
CONFERENCE OF MONTREAL

The publication of this book has been made possible through the financial contribution of the Canadian Council on Learning.

Education, Training and Sustainability

*Conditions for success
in a changing world*

Contributors:
Jérôme Bindé • Paul Cappon • Andrew Ferrier
Angel Gurría • Donald Kaberuka • Jean Lemierre
Dennis Meadows • Madeleine Meilleur • Gérard Mestrallet
Christine Ockrent • Gil Rémillard • Lucie Sauvé
Rosalía Arteaga Serrano • Michèle S. Jean

TABLE OF CONTENTS

PREFACE

Every day, we see warning signs that our way of life is endangering the planet. The Conference of Montreal of June 2008 devoted a full day to the question of sustainable development and the need to find innovative ways of eliminating polluting activities. This book provides important insights for a better understanding of both the dangers we face and the solutions that can help us resolve this crisis.

Paradoxically, the more we discuss these imminent dangers realistically, the more we risk speaking in terms to which the public will become inured, causing them to "tune out" and no longer react. We must do more than simply condemn certain ways of doing things, looking for innovative solutions that will change what we are doing: we must also find new means of informing, educating and training our citizenry about the realities of sustainable development.

That is the primary goal of this book, which brings together presentations by senior executives from international organizations and the world of business, along with researchers directly engaged in the quest for sustainability. The Conference of Montreal took place in June, at the very start of the 2008 financial crisis. We have not yet, as these words are being written, acquired sufficient perspective to properly judge the consequences of this crisis and its impact on the issues involved in sustainable development.

Nonetheless, it is clear that the downfall of "cowboy capitalism" will have profound implications for sustainable development. The impact of this crisis upon the financial capacities of our governments, organizations, businesses and ordinary citizens will force us to rethink our ways of producing and living. But how? Will this major world-wide economic slowdown make us more concerned with sustainability or will it, on the contrary, create an even harsher reality than the present one, imposing even more restrictive rules of behaviour or, worse, the brutal rules of survival?

One thing is certain. We must be especially vigilant as to the consequences this financial crisis may have on sustainable development because it will put constraints, for some time to come, on the financial capacities of all levels of decision-making. This is not the ideal situation in which to call for new ways of reducing pollution that may require major investments. That is true for our governments, which must foresee budget deficits to soften the impact of reduced revenues. It is equally true for our businesses, which are subject to the constraints of shareholder profitability and, consequently, of productivity and international competition. We must therefore make a greater effort to convince businesses that they are ensuring their own sustainability by putting in place new systems of production to protect and ensure environmental quality.

This is where information about sustainability comes into play. It must be conveyed at national and international levels by governments and by such relevant organizations as, among others, UNESCO and the OECD, both of which have been involved with the production of this book.

Furthermore, the moment is ripe to insist on governments' obligations, since their role is currently undergoing a profound transformation. Indeed, the financial crisis will have the positive effect of forcing us to return to the idea that the primary role of the State is to ensure quality public services for its population. In this regard, the end of "amoral and lawless" neo-liberalism can only be beneficial for sustainability. Without going back to the 'nanny state' of the 1960s, it is vital to strike a proper balance between over-regulation and a disastrous laissez-faire approach. All the more so, considering how information is travelling with ever greater ease and speed around the world thanks to new technologies. This forces governments to become transparent, in spite of themselves. We are living through a communications revolution that may trigger a global awareness of sustainable development among the citizens of the world. This will have immediate consequences, not only in terms of our daily living and consuming habits, but also with regards to the means and modes available for citizens to put pressure on their governments and business.

The governments and businesses of the industrialized world, like those of the emerging and developing countries, will have no choice but to take into account the reactions of well-informed citizens. Governments will do this because they can be voted in or out of office. Businesses will do so because of the pressure that consumers can exert on them to respect sustainability. The same will be true with regard to major investors, many of whom are demanding increasing respect for sustainability before they agree to invest in a company or project. The financial crisis and the subsequent economic slow-down will make information even more important as the key to raising awarencss, which is necessarily the cornerstone of sustainability.

Training and education are also two equally important aspects of this new sustainability consciousness. As Paul Cappon, President and CEO of the Canadian Council on Learning, has written with great insight: education and training form the basis of a sustainable society. "The updating and improvement of the training of teachers and trainers are essential elements of a sustainable educational system," he insists. This involves, first of all, providing high-quality, accessible and universal lifelong public education and training to all citizens.

We must also develop greater teacher and trainer awareness of the learning disabilities that afflict more and more children. The problems of dyslexia and attention deficit disorder, in particular, create intolerable obstacles for many children, who end up having no choice but to "drop out" of educational systems from which they feel excluded. This has huge social consequences. "Dropping out" takes a terrible human toll, resulting in broken lives for thousands of young people, leading all the way to suicide in some cases. A recent study by the highly respected Quebec economist Pierre Fortin puts the cost of each Quebec dropout at approximately $500,000.

In developing countries, the economic slowdown will have a significant impact on the demand for raw materials, which, just a few months ago, were still believed to be about to lift these countries out of poverty. This downturn is likely to have a huge negative impact on education and training, although they are key development factors. Moreover, due to the economic slowdown, rich countries will be less able to provide assistance. We must therefore be vigilant, especially with regard to Africa, so as to maintain education and training as overriding priorities in the coming years. Projects such as the United Nations' "Millennium Villages" developed by economist Jeffrey Sachs, Director of the *Earth Institute* at Columbia University, deserve to receive all the aid required in order to keep improving Africa's educational systems, along with its public health services and agricultural production.

This book therefore highlights the fact that education and training are still one of the most vital issues for mankind. Fortunately, important steps have been taken in the last few years towards creating a 'knowledge society' that will lead to an understanding of every aspect of sustainability. Nevertheless, the financial crisis of 2008, one of the worst economic crises since the great depression of the 1930s, may slow down the progress we have just begun to see emerge in the thinking and attitudes of all levels of government, as well as businesses and individuals. On the other hand, this crisis and the attendant economic slowdown just might have a positive side, as we return the State to its central role—a move that may prove beneficial to sustainability by giving back to our governments their inherent duty to protect the environment.

Under the pretext of economic globalization, the State has indeed been sidelined, especially in the last twenty years, by an almost limitless neo-liberalism. Today, faced with the failure of the laissez-faire approach, the State must step in and save the day. Many governments will have to make major investments in their public service providers to keep them from going bankrupt. Governments will therefore be in an excellent position to oversee the best management practices in the boardrooms, and demand new and more ethical standards of corporate behaviour and greater concern for sustainability.

All of this presupposes, of course, that States will take a hard line on sustainability. This is where citizens can play a decisive role, provided they are well informed and they know how to use effective pressure tactics to force elected officials to act responsibly.

The goal of this book is to provide useful and accessible information in order to create a better understanding of the stakes involved in sustainable development. I would like to thank the authors who agreed to allow us to publish the presentations given on June 10, 2008 at the Conference of Montreal.

The International Economic Forum of the Americas, which produces the Conference of Montreal annually, is a non-governmental organization, working in partnership with UNESCO. Each year, in this capacity during the Conference, the Forum presents "21st Century Talks," from which certain presentations are chosen for publication in book form. I wish to thank the Director-General of UNESCO, Koïchiro Matsuura, for the confidence he has shown in our organization of this event.

The International Economic Forum of the Americas/ Conference of Montreal is also a *Knowledge Partner* of the OECD, which is involved in the Forum every year. I would like to thank the Secretary-General of the OECD, Angel Gurría, for his vital cooperation, as well as John West, the Head of Public Affairs and Director of the OECD Forum, for his invaluable advice on the publication of this book.

Finally, the publication of this book would not have been possible without the participation of the Canadian Council on Learning and its President and CEO, Dr. Paul Cappon, to whom I wish to express my sincere gratitude and that of the

Board of Governors of the International Economic Forum of the Americas.

Gil RÉMILLARD

Gil Rémillard is Founding Chairman of the International Economic Forum of the Americas / Conference of Montreal, Professor at the École nationale d'administration publique du Québec (ÉNAP), and Counsel to the law firm Fraser Milner Casgrain LLP.

Education: Prerequisite for a Sustainable Society

Dr. Paul Cappon
President and CEO of the Canadian Council on Learning (CCL)

> *"Education is a human right, a basic component of open democratic and equitable societies, and essential for sustained social and economic development. Basic education and the acquisition of skills and knowledge are understood to be the main driver in reducing poverty and in sustainable development."*
>
> — Canadian International Development Agency (CIDA), Sustainable Development Strategy: 2007-2009

Lifelong education and learning—formal, informal, individual and social—are fundamental in the pursuit of a sustainable world. Over countless generations, humanity has developed the perceptions, mores, cultural guidelines and social constraints that make it possible to live together—and resolve disputes concerning access to the scarce resources of the Earth—in a civil manner at the scale of a small and personal sustainable community. Now, through education of all kinds at all stages of life, humanity must learn to extend that tacit knowledge to a global scale in a manner that can be effective in a complex, highly interdependent mesh of impersonal institutions.

The conduct of individuals, and the exercise of individual volition, is shaped by cultural foundations and an accumulation of stories that address social dilemmas and ethical imperatives. The role of education and learning in the emergence of a sustainable society, ensuring a sustainable earth for generations to come, is to build those foundations and meet that test.

The fundamental role of education in human and social development is recognized in a multitude of international conventions, beginning with the 1948 UN Universal Declaration of Human Rights and reaffirmed in subsequent agreements, including the International Covenant on Economic, Social and Cultural Rights, the Convention on the Rights of the Child, and the Convention for the Elimination of all Forms of Discrimination Against Women.

The reasons are well documented—education saves lives. It allows people to escape poverty, live in healthier conditions and acquire the means to participate fully in their communities. It reduces child mortality and helps limit the spread of HIV/AIDS. It provides women and men with the means to exercise their civil, political, economic and social rights.

In short, education is a key agent of social change, providing individuals with the tools to achieve their own social and economic well-being and to contribute to the well-being and development of their communities.

Sustainability began largely as an environmental concept, demanding that we draw on our physical environment in a way that leaves it as productive and resilient as before. It has now expanded to include the social and economic infrastructure that determines a society's capacity to sustain itself in a rapidly changing global environment. Early discourse was characterized by an assumption that development and sustainability goals were often in conflict. Despite the growing evidence of their congruity, research on both environmental and social sustainability still advances on separate, if parallel, tracks. (Policy Research Initiative, *Horizons*, 2004)

Social sustainability has both an individual and a community aspect. Investments in each enhance social capital, i.e. the skills, creativity, networks, shared values and cooperative political institutions that lead to effective decisions. Socially sustainable development adds to, rather than erodes, the store of social capital on which a society's progress depends. Social sustainability underpins a society's capacity to ensure environmental sustainability.

Social sustainability involves the interrelationship of three ideals: the stewardship of our biosphere; the crafting of an economic paradigm that conserves the planet's resources; and systems of human well-being where harmony with nature and harmony with one another are paramount.

EDUCATION'S ROLE IN ACHIEVING GLOBAL SOCIAL SUSTAINABILITY

In this way, education and social sustainability go hand in hand.

Recognizing this essential role of education in social sustainability, development and poverty reduction, the World Education Summit in Dakar, Senegal in 2000 set out six goals in Education for All:

- Expand and improve early childhood care and education;
- Provide free and compulsory universal primary education by 2015;
- Equitable access to learning and life-skills programs;
- Achieve a 50% improvement in adult literacy rates;

- Eliminate gender disparities in primary and secondary education by 2005 and at all levels by 2015; and
- Improve all aspects of the quality of education.

Examining the literature and reviewing the data on the state of education and learning today would lead many to assume that global promises such as these have been hollow. Indeed, world leaders would be hard-pressed to boast that the promise of Education for All first made in the UN's 1948 Declaration of Human Rights has been fulfilled in any sense, let alone the parallel and equally compelling pledge for an education that promotes understanding, tolerance and friendship among nations.

The record is disappointing. The 2008 edition of UNESCO's Education for All Global Monitoring Report finds: while primary school enrolment is up, 72 million children—two-thirds of them girls—still had no access to primary education in 2005; an estimated 98% of children with disabilities in developing countries do not attend school; one in five adults around the world—two-thirds of them women—lack basic literacy skills; more than 50 countries will not achieve universal primary education by 2015; more than 90 countries will fall short of gender parity in primary and secondary education by 2015, and cost remains a major obstacle to primary schooling for millions of children.

The data represent an unacceptable loss of human potential for the individuals concerned, their families, their children, their societies, and the global economy. They also constitute a continuing impediment to social and environmental sustainability.

The UNESCO report uncovers further cause for concern. It finds that the international community's emphasis on primary education has come at the expense of early childhood education and literacy programs for youth and adults. Research by the Canadian Council on Learning (CCL) demonstrates that, along with that of UNESCO and others around the world, education cannot be confined to the realm of formal public education in the early years of life. Sustainable societies demand a life-long approach that enables their citizens to take advantage of formal as well as informal opportunities for learning. While free primary education is a core human right, secondary, post-secondary and vocational education—as well as lifelong learning—are all equally critical to sustainable development. They provide the stream of qualified people who diversify economic development, develop science and technology, deliver public services, create local responses to development issues, and become enlightened leaders.

GLOBALIZATION, SUSTAINABILITY AND EDUCATION

Globalization is both a threat to and a resource for sustainability. The challenge is to maximize its benefits and minimize its negative effects.

The State of the World Forum's Commission on Globalization created a special task force called the Policy Action Group on Learning (www.paglearning.org), of which I am chair, to examine the many issues surrounding the impact of globalization on learning—all of which have a direct impact on the development of sustainable societies. The PAGL has developed a network of organizations, including UNESCO, to address a number of thematic areas. These include:

- The impact of information and communications technologies on learning in the new century;
- The roles of the private sector in forging new educational partnerships;

- The examination of the challenges and opportunities involved in cultural and linguistic preservation;
- The promotion of human rights and civic education as key elements for building peace;
- The examination of some of the issues surrounding education for sustainable development;
- The exploration of new ways of promoting lifelong learning through both formal and informal means; and
- The examination of issues concerning the development of new learning material and teacher training.

COORDINATING ACTION— MULTILATERAL INSTITUTIONS AND OTHER PARTIES

Education for All by 2015 is the second of the UN's eight Millennium Development Goals. Education is a priority in the programs of all the major multilateral institutions, from UNESCO and UNICEF to the World Bank, the European Community, and the OECD and in the Overseas Development Assistance (ODA) programs of major donor countries. While these organizations may have agreed on the Millennium Goals, they often differ on how to achieve them. The need for coordination between and among external actors and national and local plans is pressing.

The international Policy Action Group on Learning seeks to act as a catalyst to clarify issues common to all actors, as well as seek ways in which they might support each other. We identify areas of obvious overlap and duplication in the interest of a more effective use of resources. We also aim to show where the different objectives of multilateral bodies may cause friction between competing principles—for example, between strictly economic objectives and the more humanistic objectives of education and learning. We encourage decision-makers of national ODA agencies to explore complementary agendas to maximize synergies. Finally, we also encourage donors to back up their support pledges for Education for All with incentives for recipient countries to "walk the talk."

Perhaps most important of all is the need to coordinate donor activities with the priorities of recipient countries.

The task of coordinator is primarily upstream in nature and that of an "honest broker." The fact that UNESCO is part of the UN system, bridging all nations, together with the fact that it plays a minor role in actual program delivery, may situate it ideally to articulate a sustainable learning strategy for the 21st century. The challenge is to ensure that it has sufficient resources to be a catalyst and play a leadership role in implementing that strategy.

GLOBALIZATION, CULTURAL AND LINGUISTIC PRESERVATION AND THE PROMOTION OF HUMAN RIGHTS

The Universal Declaration of Human Rights, adopted by the world's nations in 1948, guaranteed that education would strengthen respect for human rights and fundamental freedoms; promote understanding, tolerance and friendship among all nations, racial and religious groups; and further the activities of the United Nations for the maintenance of peace.

Education, *per se*, does not guarantee human rights, yet the right to an education cannot be separated from the obligation to ensure that education be in the service of humanity and respect for human rights. It has to be said that the education systems in both North and South still fall short of that commitment.

How can we rectify that? Respect for human rights is not an "add-on" to other educational programming, but must permeate it. In the North, it is important not to allow a focus on the "world of work" to undermine the need to foster broader humanistic goals—an awareness of human rights, civic values and active citizenship. The Dakar pledge of advancing "learning to live together" deserves equal prominence in education in the North and South alongside "learning to know" and "learning to do."

Among those human rights is the right to pursue an education in one's own cultural context and language. Preservation of diversity is essential to mobilizing the contribution of all citizens in a sustainable society. Standardization of the language of learning threatens distinct cultures, from those of Aboriginal peoples in the North to minority cultures in the South. There is no "one-size-fits-all" solution; the sharing of effective practices from around the world will help us achieve a level of cultural sustainability consistent with each country's national objectives.

MANAGING THE DICHOTOMY BETWEEN INDIVIDUAL AND SOCIAL LEARNING GOALS

Education policy, particularly in countries pursuing rapid economic development, often emphasizes the economic goals and benefits of learning, while giving lip service to the holistic notion of education as a path to individual self-actualization. Both are important, and balancing the demands of the two is a challenging task; however, fulfilling the promise of all four "pillars of learning"—*Learning to know, Learning to do, Learning to live together* and *Learning to be*—requires nothing less, as the primary role of education itself is at stake.

Some cast the discussion in terms of education's role in sustainable human development: is it to focus on labour market preparedness, or to aim at expanding a society's intellectual capacities? If the short-term goal is primarily economic, will that emphasis create long-term barriers in seeking to move to a broader, more humanistic vision?

Within some developing countries, it may be naïve to assume that training an unending stream of marginally qualified workers will engender economic opportunities that provide them all with jobs. Research in the North and South suggests that education may encourage rural-to-urban migration that cannot be supported by the urban economy. This, rather than contributing to sustainability, results in substantial numbers of people being uprooted and worse off than before. Involvement of the private sector and local communities in education planning could bring about a better fit between opportunities and educational content at regional and national levels.

The balance between social and individual educational objectives regarding higher education is also an issue. What relative weight should be given to technical vocational education and training and workforce-related higher education, versus the intellectual development of learners for self-actualization? These are very real issues for the North today. While no definitive answer exists to these kinds of questions, the problem is universal and all education systems, North and South, will have to face it.

LIFELONG LEARNING AND INFORMAL LEARNING

In a rapidly changing, interrelated global economy, the commonly held notion of education as confined to the formal primary, secondary and post-secondary school systems—chiefly serving children and young adults—is no longer appropriate. Educators around the world now advocate a lifelong learning approach. Recognizing that learning beyond formal schooling is essential to upgrading skills and fostering the adaptability a modern economy demands, education planners seek new partnerships and venues to make Education For All a reality.

It is natural that the Millennium Goals and the Dakar commitments emphasize universal access to elementary schooling for all children; however, they also acknowledge the need to open the doors of basic learning and skills upgrading to adults if we are to attain sustainable societies. Failure to envision education as a lifelong pursuit runs the risk of creating a generational *knowledge divide*, marginalizing adults who might otherwise make a critical contribution to the achievement of sustainability.

The knowledge divide is a threat in both the North and South. In Canada, for example, it is evident in the fact that two in five Canadians lack the numeracy and literacy skills to function fully and productively in the modern economy. Another example for the North lies in the challenge of meeting the educational needs of the disabled and the elderly. Addressing the knowledge divide means involving new partners (community-based organizations, for example) and tailoring programs to the particular needs of the excluded. This is new, but essential, territory.

Lifelong learning and the pursuit of inclusive and sustainable education mean recognizing the role of informal learning: in the workplace, community and family, and outside conventional educational venues. Traditional educational infrastructures in the North and South are poorly equipped to meet the needs of adult learners. New approaches recognize that a broad spectrum of skills development takes place in private and non-profit environments, and involves new collaboration with the public sector.

SUSTAINING LEARNING RESOURCES

In proposing new approaches to education for a sustainable society, it is important to address *how* we bring this about. Programs to improve teacher training and educational practice should accompany the Dakar goals. Achieving those goals will be impossible without mobilizing the resources to build—nation by nation—the network of teachers and trainers capable of spreading learning in both traditional and non-traditional manners, and in ways that are sensitive to unique environments and challenges. Best practices, the latest developments in teacher training, and scientific findings about how people learn, must all be brought to the attention of decision-makers for implementation.

The challenges of global capacity-building should not be underestimated, nor is it a short-term investment. The maintenance and improvement of teacher and trainer development are crucial components of a sustainable education system.

Such long-term commitment also involves articulating standards and setting benchmarks against which to measure progress toward educational goals, plus an effective quantitative and qualitative assessment process. This process can draw on growing experience with social and human development outcome mapping by organizations like Canada's International Development Research Centre. Convincing decision-makers of the value of a regular assessment of education outcomes and, therefore, of the importance of investing in such assessments, is part of the challenge. Donors have a role to play in this respect.

Conclusion

A sustainable environment has long been the goal of the UN and other major bodies. As our understanding of the pre-conditions for sustainability has grown, the importance of a sustainable social infrastructure has also become obvious. In this paper, we have argued that a key element in achieving social sustainability is an inclusive sustainable education system, one that truly meets the criterion of Education for All. Learning is *the* prerequisite in seeking responsible answers to underlying questions for sustainability, such as the following: why, for example, can we not stop threatening our own and our grandchildren's life-support systems? Why can we apparently not exercise stewardship properly?

We have sketched some of the issues that must be addressed as we pursue sustainable education in both North and South. Our task is complicated and the challenges are many. We cannot afford to fail. What will sustain us as we join together in this quintessentially human endeavour is the abundant evidence for the beneficial impact of education on our lives.

I acknowledge with gratitude the comments and contributions made by Professor Rod Dobell on an earlier draft and his paper entitled *Holarchy, Panarchy, Coyote and Raven: Creation Myths for a Research Program*, Rod Dobell, March 31, 2008.

1

Sustainable Development, Innovation and Competitiveness: Squaring of the Circle or a Virtuous Circle?

Jérôme Bindé
Director of the Division of Foresight at UNESCO

> *We have inherited only one planet. And what have we done with it? Our inheritance has become endangered and the human race itself is in jeopardy.*

UNESCO, which is playing an active role in the Decade of Education for Sustainable Development, recently published *Making Peace with the Earth*,[1] the third anthology in the *21st Century Talks* series. With the collaboration of more than 15 senior scientists, experts, thinkers and political officials from the various regions of the world, we took what could be called an X-ray preview of the world ecological crisis in order to come up with a few proposals.

I will not dwell on the diagnosis. Climate change, desertification, world water crisis, deforestation, oceanic degradation, air, soil, water and sea pollution, rapid erosion of biodiversity: sadly, we already know the picture.

---

1. *Making Peace with the Earth* (2007) was published in English (Berghan Books/UNESCO), in French *Signons la paix avec la Terre* (Albin Michel/UNESCO), and in Spanish (*Firmemos la Paz con la Tierra*, Icaria/UNESCO).

The economic and geopolitical consequences of this situation are only beginning to be quantified. Our war against the planet could cost as much as a world war, as per the *Stern Report*. And, after the war against nature, is it not likely that there will be outright war, due to the growing shortage of fossil fuel and natural resources and the 150 to 200 million eco-refugees predicted in futurist studies?

But let us make no mistake: as grim as it may be, this diagnosis is only a list of symptoms. In fact, mankind's real problem is its development, which has nothing sustainable about it. More specifically, the problem is one of material growth in a finite world, raised as early as 1972 in *Limits to growth*,[2] a report presented to the Club of Rome. According to Dennis Meadows, co-author of the report, the difference now is that, "whereas in 1972 we were comfortably below the carrying capacity of the globe ... now we're significantly above." In 1972, we were at 85% of that carrying capacity. Today, human consumption of resources is around 125% of the level sustainable over the long term.

So, Can the Human Race Still Be Saved?

In *Making Peace with the Earth*, we do not hesitate to say yes it can. But to save the planet and the human race without halting human progress and the battle against poverty, growth and sustainable development must be brought into harmony instead of being in conflict.

But how? It will take more science, more restraint, fewer materials, and more of what is tangible. In other words, we will

---

2. Donella H. Meadows, Dennis L. Meadows, Jorgen Randers, and William W. Behrens III, *The Limits to Growth* (1972), Universe Books.

have to embark on a path towards a type of development that is truly sustainable and shared.

More science

Many are those who think: "Technoscience, that is the enemy!" But the hand that wounds can also heal. We will not be able to save the planet and its most important occupant, the human race, unless we build "knowledge societies" founded on education, research, new technologies, futurology, and innovation in every field.

As for UNESCO, for decades now it has been envisioning a world founded on environmental knowledge and sustainable development, going back to a time when few people were aware of the problem. As early as 1949, UNESCO launched the first international study on arid areas; in 1970 it created the international "Man and the Biosphere" (MAB) program and the Worldwide Network of Biosphere Reserves; and as for our worldwide scientific programs on the oceans and geosciences, these are unanimously recognized as being irreplaceable assets.

More restraint

We will have to *curtail overconsumption*, especially in the North, and reduce our ecological footprint. Indeed, what other choice do we have? At least three or four planet Earths would be needed if the whole planet were to consume as much as North America does today. We are now at the moment of truth, with the boom in emerging economies, their massive access to consumption and the impact of this situation, already quantifiable in terms of the food crisis and higher prices for raw materials and fossil fuel.

Fewer materials

We will have to disconnect the economy and growth from the material. For, can growth be stopped? Probably not. So what else can we do? That is what Mostafa Tolba suggests in *Making Peace with the Earth*: to produce while consuming less energy, metal or ore, water or wood. This economic shift toward the intangible has already begun, with a revolution that is replacing atoms with *bits*, and which is presiding over the expansion of new technologies and knowledge societies. Moreover, if the countries of the North would commit to dematerializing a bit more than the South for about 50 years, such dematerialization could facilitate development in the countries of the South and reduce world inequality.

Condorcet already had this wonderfully visionary idea when he wrote, over two hundred years ago, in his famous *Sketch for a Historical Picture of the Progress of the Human Mind*: "Then a smaller and smaller area of land will be able to produce commodities of greater use or higher value; wider enjoyment will be obtained with less outlay; the same manufacturing output will call for less expenditure of raw materials or will be more durable."[3] As we can see, it was Condorcet who invented sustainable development, two hundred years before the Brundtland Report. However, unlike so many experts and authorities, he did not believe it was incompatible with innovation and competitiveness. To him, there was a strong bond between sustainable development, productivity and innovation.

---

3. Marie-Jean-Antoine de Caritat Condorcet, *Esquisse d'un tableau historique des progrès de l'esprit humain* (1792), Librairie philosophique J. Vrin (1970), "Dixième époque : Les progrès futurs de l'esprit humain" (English version: *Sketch for a Historical Picture of the Progress of the Human Mind.*)

More tangibility

To close the gap between Utopia and short-term tyranny, we need tangible and realistic projects. The great scientist Edward O. Wilson provides us with one example in our work: biodiversity. The 34 ecological zones considered a priority (several contain UNESCO "biosphere reserves") cover only 2.3% of the planet's land surface, but are home to 50% of the known species of vascular plants and 42% of the mammals, birds, reptiles and amphibians. It is therefore possible to preserve them. It would cost around $50 billion, which is less than 0.1% of the world's GDP. That is almost a modest figure knowing how essential biodiversity is to life cycles, human health, our food security, as well as rendering invaluable services to the economy. Considering that it would only take 2.5% of the world's military expenditures to preserve those islands of biodiversity, what can one conclude other than that the investment fund for the apocalypse is more prosperous than the one for life?

We must change our accounting logic, for rational, fair and coordinated management of the planet is essential to ensure real sustainable development. There can be no sustainable development without a truly worldwide awareness of how urgent it is to change our habits, lifestyles, and current consumption methods. "Urgent" must be understood to mean gravity, not "emergency logic," for what is urgent is precisely the need to evolve beyond emergency logic by finally establishing long-term sustainable development. From this perspective the UNESCO World Report, *Towards Knowledge Societies,* puts the focus of tomorrow's thinking and policies on the concept of knowledge-based or knowledge societies.[4]

TOWARDS KNOWLEDGE SOCIETIES

From this point of view, it is a priority to invest in lifelong education for all, in innovation and fundamental research, in new technologies and info-development, and in equitable learning societies. Knowledge societies will be the best asset for learning about sustainable development, for they will make it possible for us to move towards, amongst other things, greater awareness of the potentially devastating effects of global warming, the promotion of a true water ethic and the global protection of biodiversity, as well as the integration of risk management in the realm of development. It will be knowledge societies that forge prognosticative tools enabling us to anticipate the dangers weighing on mankind; knowledge societies, finally, that will resolve the problems of sustainable development at an acceptable cost.

I can already hear the objections raised by some: aren't such knowledge societies a dream, a Utopia? Is this not the latest trend of the "reporting society"?

We at UNESCO do not think so: indeed, many indications let us suppose that we are truly at the dawning of a new age—the age of information and knowledge. The scientific revolutions of the 19th century, then the third industrial revolution of the 20th century—that of the new technologies—gave rise to a knowledge-based economy that puts knowledge and education at the centre of human activity, development and social change.

---

4. UNESCO World Report, *Towards Knowledge Societies* (*Hacia las Sociedades del Conocimiento*; *Vers les sociétés du savoir*) UNESCO, 2005 (http://unesdoc.unesco.org/images/0014/001418/141843e.pdf).

Of course, information is not knowledge, and knowledge has always been the basis of technical progress and the development of communication. But today we are witnessing the weaving of planetary networks, a powerful link between information and knowledge. In UNESCO's view, the global information society that is incubating—an information society which, moreover, is still not global enough—will only have real meaning if it fosters the emergence of knowledge societies that are pluralistic and participatory, inclusive rather than exclusive.

The current revolution, which is indissolubly technological and cognitive, has two profoundly original characteristics. The first is the unprecedented increase in the cataloguing of knowledge due to the information revolution, and its direct link to industry, the economy and innovation. Manuel Castells, philosopher and author of *The Rise of the Network Society*, the first volume of *The Information Age*,[5] identifies a second distinct characteristic: specifically, that what characterizes the current technological revolution is not so much the preponderant role of knowledge and information as it is their application to the processes of the creation of knowledge and the processing or dissemination of information. This creates "a cumulative feedback loop between innovation and the uses of innovation."[6]

Moreover, education, science, information, communication and culture, in other words, UNESCO's fields of expertise, still seemed in the past (no doubt mistakenly) to be relatively separate entities. Today, their strategic importance to the future of human societies is obvious: henceforth they will be the key development factors. But it is their interaction

---

5. Manuel Castells, *The Information Age: Economy, Society and Culture, Vol. 1, The Rise of the Network Society.* Malden, Mass./Oxford, Blackwell 1996.
6. *Ibid.*

and their very interpenetration that are also increasingly strategic. In that sense, one could say that knowledge societies are societal networks that "conduct" knowledge, that decompartmentalize the various sectors of intellectual, learning or knowledge activities.

SHARED OR POLARIZED KNOWLEDGE AND WEALTH?

Does that mean that the 21st century will see the development of shared-knowledge societies? As underlined in the UNESCO World Report, no one should be excluded from knowledge societies, since knowledge is a public asset that should be available to all.

However, one cannot reject out of hand the argument raised by those who believe there is a good risk the knowledge economy will reinforce the polarization on the planet of prosperous centres, be they the countries of the North or emerging countries with their skills, knowledge and wealth versus, on the margins, those that are impoverished, disconnected and without resources. A good number of economists and investigators think from this perspective that, as was the case in the 19th century with the railroad and the telegraph, which saw a new reduction in costs of transportation and communication caused by the third industrial revolution—the development of networks and the new phase of globalization that goes along with them, will reinforce the polarization of wealth, knowledge and skills around a few very localized centres on the globe, with the countries of the South irretrievably left behind in the race to the knowledge-based economy.

One must take this polarization argument into account, but without seeing it as inevitable. Knowledge can indeed be a powerful lever in the fight against poverty and under-development.

Take the example of Villa el Salvador, a Peruvian city that sprang from the desert in 1971 on the initiative of a few thousand people from the shantytowns of Lima. With no outside help, these inhabitants are building houses, roads, educational centres; they are forming associations. Despite all its handicaps, Villa el Salvador's resolute participatory development action, with women's associations playing a major role, has gradually turned this shantytown into an organized city. In 1987, the Municipal Council created the Free University of Villa El Salvador. Today, 98% of the children are educated there and the rate of adult illiteracy (4.5%) is the lowest in the country. The city has over fifteen thousand students. The municipality has invested in information technologies and every resident, now connected to the Internet, can voice his opinions on topical issues. Villa el Salvador is the laboratory for a new type of associative and participatory democracy.

This example is far from isolated, for in every part of the world a number of countries are in the process of transforming themselves and promoting a new style of development—one that is based on knowledge. The Villa el Salvador example shows how outstanding development can take place in two generations, in a city built out of nothing, which has invested in knowledge, education, and new technologies.

I could just as well have mentioned other examples of cities, territorial and local communities, or countries in the various regions of the world whose experience is worth highlighting. The development of knowledge societies can be an opportunity for emerging countries and the well-being of their populations. The example of a certain number of countries of the

South shows that massive investment in education and scientific research over several decades can reduce absolute poverty in a very major way.

Today we are therefore well aware that the development of knowledge societies, with truly shared knowledge, is the avenue that will make it possible to effectively fight poverty and avert major health disasters such as pandemics, reduce the terrible human losses from tsunamis and tropical storms, and promote humane and sustainable development. Because new development styles are now within our reach: they will no longer be founded on "blood, toil, tears and sweat," to quote Churchill, but on intelligence, a scientific and technical ability to deal with problems, an added intellectual value and the expansion of services in every sector of the economy.

But without a real forward-looking attitude, there can be no sustainable development. Our disastrous propensity to only examine events over a very short time frame must be overcome. For the first time in history, mankind must make decisions about the species and its future: populations must behave like a State. It is just as much the scale of action—at once global and local—that we must alter, as it is the time frame, henceforth defined by an awareness of the fragility, not to mention the mortality, of the human race, and of society, indeed the planet. In this field, the development of a forward-looking democracy combining representative democracy, participatory democracy and associative democracy is essential. Faced with the major problems presented by sustainable development, it will become increasingly important to have forecasts to light the way.

It is a forward-looking democracy that we must now edify—a democracy that equips itself with prognosticative tools for politicians and that integrates long-term vision in our present-day decisions—if we are to acquire the means to anticipate strategic changes and enter a virtuous circle that unites sustainable development, competitiveness and innovation.

2

Settling Social Issues Through Education and Training

ANGEL GURRÍA
Secretary-General, Organisation for Economic Co-operation
& Development (OECD)

The Organisation for Economic Co-operation & Development (OECD) counts on education and training for many of the solutions to society's challenges.

Education and training are the foundations of human development, innovation, growth and competitiveness. Higher education plays an obvious and direct role because universities have traditionally been the cradles of research-led innovations for the benefit of the society. In the context of today's globalized world, the sources of innovation are expanding in many directions. However, there is no doubt that higher education systems facilitate greater understanding of sustainable development at both global and local levels.

EDUCATION AND THE COMMON GOOD FROM AN INTERNATIONAL PERSPECTIVE

The OECD is working with UNESCO on a system to make it easier to compare international educational standards and levels in universities across borders. Education is increasingly becoming an instrument of international public good as well as a traded service. Higher education in major centres around the world is becoming more transportable and it is enabling cutting-edge research to be applied to local situations.

For example, the University of Nottingham in the United Kingdom recently established a centre of sustainable energy technology in the People's Republic of China. It supports research, teaching and learning in the field of sustainable urban development. This sophisticated research can be translated into practical, energy-efficient, and affordable solutions for residential and business construction in China.

At the same time, the OECD is working with the Environment Minister of China and has made recommendations for environmental policy and sustainability. The Chinese government now is following some of the recommendations, already having expanded its Environment Protection Agency into a full ministry.

Schools and other learning centres have crucial roles in furthering sustainable development. Being virtually universal, schools are the ideal system through which one generation can transmit knowledge and learning to the next. Sustainable development exemplifies the notion of intergenerational responsibility.

The OECD examines this issue all the way from the cradle through all levels of education. Some issues have to be taught throughout life. A seminar in Washington on financial education and financial culture concluded that people have to have some education in finance to be self-sufficient; for example, a basic knowledge of mortgages, simple investments, and so on. They do not have to be specialists in finance in order to lead everyday lives. Another issue that requires lifelong education and input is sustainability. Managing the elements of the environment is closely intertwined with the questions of the social side of sustainability.

THE PROGRAM FOR INTERNATIONAL STUDENT ASSESSMENT

The OECD helps national education authorities to address emerging challenges such as the need to boost scientific knowledge and the need for increasing sensibility and knowledge about climate change. The OECD's program is called the Program for International Student Assessment (PISA). It evaluates education by assessing the scientific, mathematical and language literacy of 15-year-olds through a survey every three years. The surveys started in 2000 and the most recent results (Dec., 2007) had sampled 20 million students in 57 countries.

The surveys examined reading and language, mathematics and science literacy. One phase of PISA questions 15-year-olds about their awareness of environmental issues and sustainability issues. The results showed that, in OECD countries, three-quarters of 15-year-olds said they were aware of the negative effects of deforestation. More than half of those had heard of acid rain, greenhouse gases and nuclear waste, and a little more than one-third were aware of the surge in genetically-modified plants and animals.

The good news is that most 15-year-olds say that they are aware of issues directly related to sustainability. Furthermore, students with high levels of scientific literacy strongly supported policies favouring responsible sustainable development. The sample is huge and the evidence suggests that education and training systems can take some of the credit for that.

However, there is a perturbing dark side to this: young people are not optimistic about the future. Only one in five surveyed thought that energy shortages would improve over the next 20 years. They were even more pessimistic about water shortages, air pollution, nuclear waste, the extinction of plants and animals, the survival of biodiversity and deforestation.

There are a number of other worrying factors:

- Students with greater scientific knowledge doubt that environmental issues are being addressed successfully.
- Students with less knowledge of science do not care about sustainable development.
- Fewer and fewer students in the world are interested in science. They want to work in an investment bank or become very high-paid athletes or musicians. Even in countries traditionally strong on science, such as Japan, few young people want to be scientists anymore.

This means that in 20 years, there will be fewer people promoting scientific innovation, and issues like sustainability will attract little attention and yield little evidence.

WHO THEN WILL TAKE CARE OF SUSTAINABLE DEVELOPMENT?

What can the education system do? A lot can be changed between the age of 15 and adulthood. Young people will expand both their academic knowledge and their belief that they can change things.

However, if that is to occur, education and training systems must increase and specifically broaden knowledge and awareness of sustainable development. Part of that effort should be teaching people about political processes, so they can be assured that their efforts and commitment to new ideas can have a positive effect on sustainable development.

How can we ensure that training and education systems will focus on sustainability? PISA surveys the general knowledge of reading, science and mathematics of teenagers; however, the awareness of sustainability and the skills to manage it have to exist in lifelong education and on-the-job training. The question of sustainability also depends a lot on what kind of skills adults have.

The OECD has launched a Program for International Assessment of Adult Competencies (PIAAC), with assistance from the Council of Ministers of Education, Canada (CMEC) on the Canadian side. It is inspired by the European model of lifelong learning and it is taking hold elsewhere. PIAAC (Program for International Assessment of Adult Competencies) helps governments evaluate and design skills so that workers and companies can be innovative, flexible and responsible. In this, the labour force, employers and the governments must cooperate.

The CCL is an example of an educational institution that is in the forefront. Its 2008 Composite Learning Index measures Canada's progress in lifelong learning. Using the same methodology, Dr. Paul Cappon, President & CEO of CCL, is now expanding the study to Europe. The CCL also has published its studies in books entitled *The State of Learning in Canada, No Time for Complacency, and Post-Secondary Education in Canada*. These are valuable research tools. At the OECD, we have analyzed the Youth Labour Market and have produced a book, *Les emplois pour les jeunes*—Jobs for Youth, so many organizations are joining forces for the benefit of education and youth in Canada and elsewhere.

The solutions to climate change and other threats to sustainable development require scientific research and development, but those solutions also need the political will to be carried out. Education and training, those two fundamental routes to critical thought, are our first and our best routes to awareness and success.

Mankind has made many errors but many of the effects can be stabilized or reversed. It is particularly important to make young people understand that they can have an impact on how the environment is cared for. A few remarkable examples of success are inspirational. Some of the most polluted rivers in North America and Europe have been cleaned up. And the hole in the ozone layer is not getting bigger as quickly, thanks to the action of government to limit chlorofluorocarbons (CFCs) in aerosols.

We did it. And we succeeded.

3

Reconciling Communication, Information Technologies and Sustainability

CHRISTINE OCKRENT

Executive Director, Société de l'audiovisuel extérieur de la France

What I find striking today in our affluent societies, is that sustainability and sustainable development are raising the stakes. True, these challenges we are facing now are not new ones—as always, we need to strive to adjust our behaviour, our institutions and educational systems, while ensuring equal opportunity and equal access to resources for all. Furthermore, typically and increasingly, this is being achieved through what is generally called "information and communication." The conundrum here is that the overwhelming technological acceleration seen in the areas of information and communication is at the same time a problem, since these technologies are energy consuming and, if not *the* solution, they are at least one of the solutions to the issue of increasing energy consumption.

CONSUMERS: THE NEW KINGS OF INFORMATION

My first point concerns the acceleration and convergence of technologies. As Eric Schmidt, chairman and CEO of Google, put it, not only has the Internet become the primary way for us all to communicate, it is also the facilitator of a new phenomenon, one in which the consumer has become more powerful than the provider.

Years ago, television used film rather than video, and had little or no access to satellites. The networks would actually compel viewers to watch their programs and decided when they should watch them.

It is the reverse today. It is the consumer who decides when and what he or she wants to watch. Is he or she more interested in sustainability in the Amazon and on the planet, or in those silly on-line games that consume more and more power? Some people say: "Oh, I'm so concerned about the Amazon" and then play poker on-line all night. And they do not realize that by doing so, they consume en masse more energy than the lighting up of entire cities in our prosperous world. Many consumers do not relate the way they behave to what they claim to be concerned about.

Politicians are always late in catching up with these phenomena. Politicians, particularly in France, often think that their citizens still believe that politicians know best: when they lose an election, they realize that it is not always the case. But it is also true that because of the global communication and information revolution, democracies are increasingly led by opinion and, therefore, by emotion, as media deal primarily with emotions.

In some ways, sustainability of the planet is also related to emotions. Al Gore, Nobel Laureate and Academy Award winner, understood this well. He used emotion to warn the world about the deterioration of the earth and its atmosphere.

Still, it is very difficult for people—both politicians and citizens—to correlate emotions with the way they behave.

Behaviour, Opinions and Emotions: The Big Gap

My second point addresses precisely this gap between our behaviour, our opinions, the emotions we feel, and the individualism, fragmentation, even tribalization of behaviour increasingly present in contemporary society, is a phenomenon both carried and strengthened by information technologies.

In this regard it will suffice to consider the huge importance of social networking sites. On Facebook for example, among its many other functions, the most accessed is "pet throwing" wherein you create a cyberspace animal and you "throw" it at politicians, stars, friends or acquaintances, for whatever reason. You want to express disapproval? Just design a little cyber dog and unleash it at someone you don't like!

On YouTube, ten hours of video content is downloaded every minute; on Google over 30 million pictures are exchanged daily. But within this monstrous proliferation of data, one finds very little real information that is measurable and verifiable. This is more about communication, albeit a type of communication that is poorly filtered and often empty.

The Web's Hidden Face

There is plenty of rubbish on the Web and one of the challenges is to avoid being immersed in it. One problem with the Web is that everybody's opinion is, in effect, as worthy as everyone else's. And so you get a lot of nonsense, especially for those who like conspiracy theories and highly controversial subjects such as the GMO (genetically modified organism) issue. The subject of GMOs is being hotly debated in France the way politics used to be debated. Does this mean that people are better informed by experts on issues like GMOs? Not necessarily. On the one hand, great progress through media and information technology has allowed many to have access to what interests them; on the other hand however, they often seek the opinions of individuals who are no better informed than they are and who simply agree with them. There is, therefore, a new tendency arising from this revolution in information and communication, one that fosters—while perhaps not illiteracy, as that would be too pessimistic—an undisciplined and even irrational approach to concerns that are of great importance and great complexity.

FOR A COLLECTIVE AWARENESS

And that will take me to my last and final point, which addresses developing awareness and behaviour emulation. What can we do to ensure that this collective growing awareness of sustainable development, as well as what is becoming known as "eco-communication," will be achieved through information and communication tools we can more efficiently control and share?

In France, a few months ago, President Nicolas Sarkozy initiated what the French media have called "The Grenelle of environment," an allusion to Grenelle street where ministerial facilities stand, vast enough to accommodate a large number of people. During several weeks of discussions on sustainable development, Jean-Louis Borloo, the minister in charge, brought together NGOs, experts, and political party representatives to try and move things forward, to transform our economies and our individual behaviour, as well as our legislation.

This is also a priority for the French Presidency of the European Union, which was assumed on July 1, 2008 for a period of six months.

It was particularly interesting, during these discussions, to note that one of the topics on which participants could not agree was how advertising should evolve. It is all very nice to discuss "sustainable development," "our planet's future," and "energy sources"… but then, you mechanically sit down in front of the TV and start zapping through channels, or go to your computer to surf the Net. On TV one is smothered by car ads, like SUVs for example, and it is easy to understand that advertising executives—incidentally, often very talented—will aim at the emotional side of potential car buyers who wish, of course, to get a "green" car. How absurd! Obviously, a car that still works on fuel or diesel cannot be dubbed ecological. As far as I know, up to now, Norway is the sole country that (since last October) imposes strict rules on advertisers, forbidding car manufacturers to use some particular adjectives. For instance, they cannot say that their car is "green," "clean," and "environmentally friendly." They cannot say that your car will actually protect the environment, because that is clearly not true.

Let us hope that these notions of eco-compatibility or eco-conception will gradually emerge in a number of important areas. I believe that advertising will be one sector in the huge field of communications that will be quite interesting to watch in this respect.

Regarding sustainable development, we are confronted with the same attitudes, somewhat hypocritical let us admit, and often very emotional and devoid of scientific reasoning. OECD Secretary General, Angel Gurría, was right when he stressed the unfortunate fact that in our society today, more boys and girls plan to work in hedge funds than undertake scientific studies, although the current financial crisis might deter them somewhat. As a direct consequence of the all-round development of information and communication networks, the world of communications is increasingly being misrepresented by statements less and less supported by facts, and more and more tainted with emotions and polemics. This problem should definitely be taken into account.

The Technological Revolution at the Service of Information and Education

One last thought about the extraordinary gap between the rich and poor societies of the world. It is interesting to note that in the Millennium goals, one of the issues of course had to do with information and communication. There was the great belief which Nicholas Negroponte of MIT, among others, encouraged: the conviction that shipping cheap computers to people in poor communities, in Africa for example, would see people actually jump ahead in terms of literacy, education and information. This optimistic take on the technological revolution is based upon the belief that access to tools of information is becoming more and more accessible.

In conclusion, two important points:

- Let us beware of the amazing technological literacy that children often demonstrate. Computers and the Internet are great tools for education, throughout life; however, the Web also manifests a strong tendency for the media, the advertising industry and bloggers to promote a growing kind of illiteracy. It is not about knowing how to read; it is about how to distinguish between what is important and what is not; what is rubbish, what is serious; what is valuable information and and what is propaganda.

- The other point concerns the emerging part of the world. The Chinese strive for a Western standard of living and there will be major difficulties, of course, in convincing them that they shouldn't have all the cars that we have, that they shouldn't indulge in all the hot water that we have, etc...and the same applies to the people of the Indian sub-continent. A large percentage of the world's population clearly long to enjoy the same standards as our own, and for them, durability may have another meaning. But of course, as with the Chinese proverb, a world crisis involves both danger and opportunity, so let us hope it is an opportunity for us all.

4

The Harsh Reality of Unsustainable Development

Rosalía Arteaga Serrano
President, Fundación FIDAL
Executive Director, Fundación Natura Regional
Former President of Ecuador
Former Secretary-General of the Amazon Cooperation Treaty
Organization (ACTO)

From the Latin-American perspective, and particularly in the Andean-Amazon region, environmental sustainability is a matter of life and death.

The Amazon region is a diverse and vast territory that nurtures life and embraces the world's largest hydrographical basin. Political divisions both connect and divide the Basin in a land where a mountain chain is the backbone of a continent. This sturdy spine spans countries with varying standards of living, some of which have not achieved a minimal level of development or acceptable living conditions.

The Amazon region is vast: seven-and-a-half million square kilometres or approximately 40% of Latin America's territory. It embraces the most complex biodiversity on the planet and almost 20% of the world's fresh water reserves. Still, surprisingly it is considered a peripheral territory even within the countries that it belongs to.

The Amazon region also represents some of the world's lowest indicators in health and education. A further challenge to sustainability is presented by, among other things, climate change brought on by the actions of human beings in that particular territory, as in the whole world.

For some people, including politicians and academics, the Amazon region appears to be a huge empty space; however, it is rich in biodiversity, forests, rivers and exotic species, and it is also inhabited by human beings, a reality less frequently acknowledged. The Amazon region is home to approximately 30 million inhabitants, the majority of whom are concentrated in major cities like Manaus, Belém, Iquitos or Santa Cruz de la Sierra. The structure and fragility of the rural Amazon territory is not conducive to a dense population that could destroy delicate ecosystems.

The Amazon: One of the Greatest Climate Regulators of the World

Conservation is not the only priority. The natural riches of the Amazon lands and waters, while a delicate eco-system of flora and fauna, also includes mineral wealth that constitutes important revenue for the countries that share its territories. The exploitation of oil, gas, gold, copper and precious stones represents crucial income, yet these activities are often at odds with the concepts of careful eco-development and sustainability in the Amazon. Striking a balance in the region is therefore a complex task, and while the citizenry hopes for adequate and advantageous life solutions, there is the need to conserve and preserve a space that is known as the lungs of humanity.

Also called humanity's air conditioning, the Amazon region certainly is one of the world's most important climate regulators. Imagine the effects on Amazon countries, and even the United States and Canada, if the forest were destroyed and the eco-system damaged. This threat is real. Amazon countries are dependent upon natural resources, the development of which profoundly affects the eco-system. In addition to the exploitation of oil, gas, gold, copper and precious stones, there is added pressure from agricultural plantations, cultivation of bio-fuels, animal husbandry and forestry. As well, on the illegal front, there is bio-piracy and the production of illicit substances like drugs. Both the Amazon people and their land and waters suffer.

Years ago there were fewer uncertainties; however, the situation appears more complex today.

Economic Disparities and Sustainable Development: Contradictory Notions

Latin America is a region where the economic disparities have been catalogued as the largest in the world. Therefore, it is a challenge to anticipate change or to formulate strategies when the goals are sometimes contradictory. Sustainable development, innovation and competitiveness are goals that we cannot ignore since our future depends on them.

The author Cristovam Buarque, a senator and former education minister of Brazil, has posed the question:

"If answers kill questions, why do questions create answers?"

We assume risk when we try to answer complex questions, but it is worth it. Latin America is a young continent and is sometimes referred to as the "continent of hope."

Buarque also asks: "Why do the young who have every-thing to lose take more risks than the old who have no future?"

YOU SAID "GLOCAL"?

There are often answers in new concepts such as *"glocal."* The term *"glocal"* suggests a possible harmony between the contradictory terms, *"global"* and *"local."* It embraces the importance of advances in science and the revolution in tech-nology and telecommunications with such innovations as the Internet, iPhone, Blackberry, U2wave 2.0, televisions and satel-lites, among others.

Other controversial developments, in biotechnology for example, aim to improve their quality of life. These develop-ments include decoding the human genetic map, cloning, and transgenic products. Not only has the world achieved global-ization on the economic level, it has also globalized telecom-munications and many other scientific advances, some positive and some negative.

There is an apparent dichotomy in the *"glocal"* syndrome, with its core philosophy of maintaining identities and culture, set against the reality of globalization. The peoples of each nation do not want to be threatened by imposed uniformity from outside. Many parts of the world are undergoing a revival of ethnicity, nationalism and an intense struggle to accommo-date religion. These movements manifest a strong desire for people to show themselves as being similar to their neighbours, but different from those who live far away. Latin Americans have always felt a part of the world, yet distinctive, representing the epitome of *"glocal."*

The idea of a successful concept of *"glocal"* would be to avoid conflicts. This blending of local and global priorities could help us sort out the complexities of the ultra-modern world of internationalism.

Is civilization a giant sadomasochistic orgy? This is another question posed by Buarque. Maybe what happens is that we do not ask the right questions and therefore cannot find adequate answers.

THE HUMAN FACTOR

The world is facing challenges so daunting that they seem to be unconquerable. Simultaneous battles rage against corruption, hunger and poverty. Now there is a new challenge—simply to produce affordable food for an increasing world population. We are having difficulty taming a world that not so long ago seemed to be under control in many fundamental aspects.

The competition for energy and the pressure of bio-fuel production, with its questionable effects on food scarcity and famine, might expand and provoke the bloodiest wars in human history.

The concern about fresh water reserves for human consumption presents us with a complex challenge; however, we can count on the human capacity of innovation and creativity to form solutions and alternatives. These solutions will arise from the inventions of wise men and women.

When we refer to wise men and women, we must look beyond those with formal educations and those who disseminate well-published knowledge. Knowledge also comes from traditional and ancient cultures. For example, in mathematics, compare *quipus*, the ancient pre-Incan method of multiplication using knotted cords, with modern calculation. As Minister of Education of Ecuador, I compared the systems with children who were bilingual in Spanish and Quichua (the language of some South American indigenous people). Those children calculated more quickly with *quipus* than with modern math. Another example is the ancient pre-Colombian method of farm cropping in terraces. Rotating the use of farm-land is more effective than the cultivation of extensive and large plantations. In the Amazon region in particular, the latter is not recommended.

Clearly, there are various routes with which to approach knowledge. It is important to keep our minds open in this world of uncertainties. Maintaining the potential to be amazed gives birth to creativity.

Basic to this are innovation, science and technology, all in the service of human beings who will share their environment with others and respect nature. That is the Gaia the ancient Greeks spoke of. The Gaia hypothesis is an ecological concept that the physical components of the earth interact in a complex system and that the planet can be viewed as a single organism.

Some academic researchers have already said the world has gone beyond what we can call point zero, a point where nothing can save the planet and humanity from a total debacle. This is a fatalism that we must fight, with both developed and non-developed countries working together. Even with the existing imbalance in societies, we still have the capacity to recover. The "collapse" to which bio-geographer and author Jared Diamond refers can be prevented. This means we can do something more than mitigate on one side and adapt ourselves on the other to the changes that are to come.

FOR A GLOBAL *MINGA*

It is important to understand that we all are in the same boat and that it is starting to sink. Our basic tool to reform all this is the concept of solidarity. The problem is that nobody can be healthy in a sick milieu.

The ancient inhabitants of America, the pre-Columbian civilizations, had a communitarian work-sharing system called *minga*. A *minga* can be defined as a collective work system. These co-operatives are still common in rural communities in Ecuador and also in Brazil, where the system is called *mutirao*.

Maybe it is time to institute a global *minga,* a co-operative work system to build a sustainable world. This would give people the solidarity and strength to battle the world's expanding crises: identity, economy, housing, food, terrorism and violence, as well as natural disequilibria such as tsunamis, hurricanes, floods and droughts.

A *minga* is useful for building a house, an irrigation channel, a road, a church or a clinic. This type of co-operation could be a foundation for the communal work needed to stabilize the planet's equilibrium and balance the needs of small and large nations, both developed and undeveloped.

5

Reconciling Sustainability with Innovation and Competitiveness

DENNIS MEADOWS
President, Laboratory for Interactive Learning, and Professor
Emeritus for Systems Policy, University of New Hampshire

Over the next 20 years, the world's industrial countries will pass through larger changes in their economies, politics, environments and cultures than they experienced during the entire previous century. The past 100 years will look relatively peaceful and stable compared to what is coming. Massive change is inevitable, but there is still time to take action that will reduce the most negative effects. The innovations that society implements now will shape those changes and will help to determine which path the world takes. But the world needs innovations in the social realm as well as new technologies.

In 1969, I joined the faculty of the management school at the Massachusetts Institute of Technology (MIT) in Boston. My goal then was to teach people how to run companies that would become competitive, innovative and profitable in the short-term.

The Limits to Growth

However, in 1972, my goals and my work changed. I received support from the Club of Rome to assemble a scientific team able to study the longer-term consequences of the policies that have produced innovation, competition and profits. To understand those consequences we built a computer model, World3. Our results were published in a book, *The Limits to Growth*, which was eventually translated into more than 30 languages.

Our conclusions were that physical growth—the rapid, worldwide expansion of population and industrial output—will end on this planet between 2010 and 2050. Climate change and fossil fuel depletion are just two of the many crises foreseen in the coming decades, as the earth strives to re-establish balance between human demands and the planet's capacities.

As pressures mount to stop current physical growth trends, there are opportunities for new technologies and a need for great leaders. But neither will be decisive. The shape of the planet's future society will depend mainly on whether its citizens can change their habits. Sustainable development will only be achieved with new habits of consumption, and that means new ethics, new economic goals and new cultural norms.

The following exercise illustrates some important insights about habit change:

1.   Cross your arms. Note which wrist is on top.

2.   Drop your arms, and then cross them a second time. Again, note which wrist is on top.

3.   Most people cross their arms in the same direction every time. Once they have developed a habit that works, they keep using it.

4. But sometimes circumstances change and old habits must be dropped in order to do something new.
5. So practice a new habit. Cross your arms again, but this time with the other wrist on top.
6. Probably you noticed three things that will also apply to society's habits in relation to physical growth:
    i)   It is possible to change an old habit.
    ii) However, it requires thought, and it may involve a few errors, until you establish a new pattern of behaviour.
    iii) It is uncomfortable at first to abandon an old habit and to do things in a new way.

RETHINKING OUR WAYS OF DOING THINGS

For almost 150 years, achieving growth has been a priority for the world's people. To be successful, citizens and leaders developed many habits, e.g. habits that governed investments, production and consumption. In our political, economic and managerial systems, society adopted practices that led to growth: more industrial output, better food, rising personal wealth. Many parts of the world were incredibly successful. And the habits became firmly established.

However, circumstances have changed. The demands of economic systems have grown above the levels that the planet can sustain over the long term. The old habits that used to produce growth now lead to collapse. The symptoms are apparent in many areas, for example, in climate change, groundwater overpumping, marine fish depletion, soil erosion and the explosion of debt.

A wise man once observed, "Trends that can't go on forever, don't." And our model showed that these trends will be stopped soon. However, the end of growth might come in one of two ways: through an orderly slowing and accommodation with the earth's limits or through overshoot and collapse.

The challenge is to discover and adopt habits that can lead global society to sustainable development. As the world's citizens adopt those new habits they will encounter the same results as they did with the simple exercise of crossing arms:

1. It is possible to change habits relating to the use of energy, environment and resources.
2. But it is going to take a lot of thought, and people will make mistakes at first.
3. Many people and organizations are going to feel unfamiliar and uncomfortable at first with the new ways of doing things.

Innovation is required for this transition, but it will be more than innovation in the technical realm; demography and culture must change as well.

KNOWING THE GOOD QUESTIONS TO ASK

When I began to ask how sustainability could be achieved, three of my ideas quickly proved to be false: (1) I assumed everyone understood the concept of sustainable development. In fact, nobody fully understands it, including me; (2) I assumed that society could achieve sustainable development without making any big changes in consumption, and that the future could be as comfortable as the past. I was wrong in this idea as well; (3) and finally, I assumed the tools to achieve sustainable development could be secured through our efforts in existing markets and through our traditional policies for developing technology. I thought that political and economic leaders would find the path to sustainability by continuing, more or less, as they had in the past. That idea also turned out to be quite false.

But What Exactly Is Sustainable Development?

Sometimes people use the phrase as if it were a destination. "How can we make this company sustainable?" "How can our country achieve sustainable development?" It is not a destination; it is not where we want to go. It is how we make the trip. Sustainability is a behaviour pattern; it is not a precise and static goal.

As a result, the notion of sustainable development has no meaning unless it is specifically linked to a particular period of time. For example, a room full of people can be sustained over the next few minutes without difficulty, but not for weeks. A city can be sustained for a few weeks without problems, but not for years. And meaningful sustainable development on a global scale involves many decades; new habits are necessary that foster a legacy for a decent life to our children, their children and the generations after that.

To describe the behaviour of complex systems, we use a variety of words, for example: stability, resilience and efficiency.

"Stability" refers to a situation in which important circumstances do not change. A stable system is one that continues steadily along a desired path.

"Resilience" is a characteristic of systems that have the ability to recover from difficult conditions such as the economic shock of a credit crisis, the tripling of oil prices or significant climate change. When a resilient system recovers it is once again able to satisfy society's goals. Non-resilient systems simply collapse and disappear after they receive a shock that pushes them outside their adaptive limits.

"Efficiency" is a measure of how much useful output is produced from the input of crucial resources. For example, we might measure fuel efficiency with an indicator of miles per gallon, or agricultural efficiency with an indicator of kilograms of wheat per gallon of irrigation water.

When people say that they are trying to achieve sustainable development, they typically are pursuing policies that could raise the stability, the resilience or the efficiency of a system. There is an inescapable social component in all this: it depends on which factors people think are most important.

Several years ago most people were not particularly concerned about energy efficiency; now they are. And soon water efficiency will become a central concern. The change reflects people's evolving perceptions.

These three characteristics of a system's behaviour—stability, resilience, and efficiency—do not refer to objective scientific standards. They are judged in relation to the goals of a society or a person or an organization. Therefore, sustainability is closely related to the ethics, culture and habits of the citizenry. One consequence of this is that sustainable development will be different from one culture to another.

Symptoms of a Big Overshoot

Whatever form it takes, sustainability will not be possible without major changes in our current material standards of living, because the current use of energy and resources is far above the level that can be supported on the planet.

Climate change and energy scarcity are not problems; they are symptoms of this overshoot. They are just two of the pressures that will inevitably arise until the habits sustaining growth in population and consumption will have been balanced.

When we wrote our first book in 1972, population and material consumption were still within the support capacity of the planet. But now these issues of physical growth are so far above that capacity that they will generate escalating problems for many future decades irrespective of society's actions today. For example, the effects of climate change and of dependence on fossil fuel oil sources will be so significant that substantial changes can no longer be avoided. Thus, we need to search for adaptive responses, policies that will reduce the impact of future changes. Both social and technical innovation will be required.

TO MEET THE ENERGY CHALLENGE THROUGH SOCIAL AND TECHNICAL INNOVATION

Global oil consumption was practically zero in 1900. About 98% of all the petroleum ever used during humanity's entire existence on this planet has occurred since 1942, the year of my birth. And depletion will bring petroleum consumption practically to zero again before 2100. The first half of this story is based on historical data. The second half is an educated guess about the future, but it is not a radical forecast. It reflects the beliefs of many geologists in the petroleum industry. Even the International Energy Agency has begun to acknowledge the likelihood of declining supply, now that the organization's analysts are forecasting the future by focusing on resource constraints rather than on energy demand trends.

Some leading oil analysts have concluded that we are already past the peak. They believe it occurred in 2006. Others think it will come in the next five years. The precise timing of the peak makes little difference, since it will take 50 years or more to develop an energy system that is not reliant on fossil energy. Unfortunately, the peaks in gas and coal production will also occur in this century. So gas and coal do not have the potential to compensate for falling oil supplies, even if they were more appealing options.

Oil production is projected to decline by almost 50% between now and 2030. You cannot consume something that you do not have. So society's consumption of oil will decline rapidly. Since oil use depends on four factors, we can say with absolute certainty that declines in oil use will occur through a combination of reductions in those four factors.

1. Population size;
2. The number of units of "capital" each person uses to support his or her lifestyle: cars, houses, light bulbs, airplanes, and related products;
3. The amount of energy required by each unit of capital; and
4. The fraction of that energy that comes from oil.

The first factor lies within the realm of demography; the second involves culture. To adapt these to the new reality, social innovations are necessary. The third and fourth factors involve technical innovations: inventions that raise energy efficiency and increase the role of non-oil energy sources.

Industrial nations have been working to improve energy efficiency and to raise the role of alternative energy. They have achieved some success. However, the steady increase in population and material living standards has counteracted those gains. Gains in energy efficiency and in the use of non-fossil energy sources have been offset by growth in population and living standards. Therefore, the demand for energy today is greater than ever before. To achieve sustainable development, attention must shift to include sociology as well as technology.

Success will require a much longer time horizon among decision makers, including politicians. Now the time perspective is short—a few months or a year—perhaps as far as the next election at most.

For some problems, actions that provide fundamental solutions over the long term also look good in the short term; for example, repairing the nation's transportation infrastructure or educating its citizens. Those are relatively easy problems to solve. Unfortunately, the issues involved in sustainability do not often behave that way. For example, there are fundamental solutions that will make energy relatively less expensive and more available over the longer term, i.e. the next several decades. However, these solutions will likely make energy seem more costly and scarce over the short term. To stay popular with the electorate and shareholders, politicians and the business marketplace will not always make the correct policy choices for these more difficult problems. Politicians are reluctant to propose solutions that impose costs on their constituents before the next election. Corporate leaders worry that solutions that might give greater sustainability over the long term will lower their stock price and reduce profits by the end of the next financial quarter.

This impasse between the need for long-term solutions and the reluctance of short-term decision makers will only be resolved when we start to demand longer-term time perspectives of our leaders and ask them to include social as well as technological innovations in their prescriptions for how we must change our habits.

6

Our Ontario Neighbours:
Education, Training and Sustainability

THE HONOURABLE MADELEINE MEILLEUR
Minister of Community and Social Services,
Minister Responsible for Francophone Affairs of Ontario

The issues of education and training as primary sources
of sustainability definitely exemplify the fact that we live in a
world without borders, within an economic system that relies
more and more upon human capital. In my opinion, sustainability and our world in transition are at the forefront of the
great socio-economic stakes of the 21ˢᵗ century.

It has been demonstrated that the foundations of sustainable development also involve training, education and all other
forms of learning. This is very positive news, as the initial aim
of the movement associated with sustainable development is
not only to salvage our environmental heritage, it is ultimately
intended to ensure human development within a protected
ecological system.

SUSTAINABLE DEVELOPMENT AND
HUMAN DEVELOPMENT

The link between environmental sustainability and
learning is reflected in the work of the great economist and

philosopher, Jane Jacobs, author of *The Economy of Cities* (1969) and *Cities and the Wealth of Nations* (1984). According to Jacobs, the dynamics governing ecosystems are similar to those governing economic systems. The interaction among the components of the system, as well as the education thereof, reinforces harmony within the system.

In Ontario, the interaction among communities and various learning modes within minority communities contribute to sustainable human development and harmony.

Today, it is critical to place sustainable development within a perspective of human development. Here I want to stress the roles played by governments and civil society to protect and promote this human heritage through learning, education and training.

My functions as Minister responsible for Francophone Affairs and Minister of Community and Social Services in the Government of Ontario naturally lead me to address three issues that are critical to me and which call for reflection. These are: sustainability and learning amongst the young, the minority Francophone community in Ontario, and the integration of newcomers in our province.

Cultural Diversity and Social Equilibrium

Canada and Ontario are young states born less than 200 years ago. Our history was nurtured by the partnership between three founding peoples. With its Native, French, and English roots, Canada is a country that, more than ever, values the flourishing of cultural diversity and full development of its constituent communities.

But Canada, including the province of Ontario, which is home to more than 40% of the nation's population, is also host to a large number of newcomers. Each year, more than 200,000 immigrants choose Canada as a new home, and more than half of them come to Ontario. Their human potential and learning capability are limitless.

I remember Jacques Delors mentioning the four pillars that support learning and sustainability. I particularly keep the fourth pillar of learning in view: the need to learn to live together, in addition to learning to know, to do and to be. Learning to live together is, in my view, the pillar that supports social harmony and ensures sustainable intercultural development.

SUSTAINABILITY AND FRANCOPHONIE: EDUCATION AND LEARNING

This leads me to mention the innovative approach Ontario has undertaken towards its minority Francophone community, which aims at endowing Francophones with tools to enable them to learn together within their own institutions, their own living environment, their family and community context.

In Ontario, we firmly believe that sustainable human development for Francophones definitely requires education and training *by* and *for* Francophones. And this concerns formal education as well as other forms of learning. Numerous examples attest clearly to the sustainability achieved in the Franco-Ontarian community thanks to systemic measures implemented by the Government.

One needs to understand that the situation of Ontario Francophones is that we form less than 5% of the province's total population, while we are spread across a territory larger than Italy. But, at the same time, Ontario Francophones benefit from full access to education in French at both elementary school and secondary school levels. Hundreds of schools are thus regrouped within school boards under the governance of Francophones.

At the post-secondary level, Ontario possesses two Francophone colleges, one dedicated to decorative arts and the other to technologies, whose learning activities are offered to the whole of Ontario. Ontario Francophones also have access to a large network of university programs in French, within a bilingual governance environment. All of these institutions, at all levels, incorporate learning activities pertaining to formal education as well as enhancing the Francophone identity. In other words, in these institutions, teaching does not solely focus on inculcating technical knowledge, but also on what it is to be a Francophone.

The experience thus initiated in the French language education sector is one of the pillars of sustainable human development in a minority community. The implementation, in 2006, of the *Aménagement linguistique* policy, or language planning policy, which aims at promoting the French language and culture and improving the performance of Francophone students, was met with success. This policy has made Ontario an example for all of Canada.

Let me also mention the large French-language immersion schools network that addresses the English-speaking majority community. In these schools, young Anglophones not only learn French, but also acquire a taste for living in French.

For the first time in Ontario history, we are witnessing the emergence of young Anglophone and bilingual leaders who were educated in these French immersion schools. The education experience continues to act as a role model for the Government and civil society in other sectors of social life.

In Ontario, services offered to Francophones function under a framework law on services in French. The various ministries are bound to incorporate within their planning a component on access to services in French for their citizens, as well as ensuring its quality. The Ontario legal system now includes a growing number of Francophone and bilingual judges. More and more professionals in the health care system have been trained to be able to treat Francophones in their language. In Ontario, we have a social and community service network focused on offering services in French, provided by Francophones.

Ontario also protects Francophone heritage through its cultural policies. Education in French for young children from French-speaking environments has become a priority in Ontario, since we understand how crucial the first years in a child's life are to the development of his/her cultural and community identity.

In our opinion, sustainability in Francophone community life is achieved when the child acquires knowledge in French, learns to do things in French, to be a Francophone, and to live in French as a full member of society. However, this example of sustainable human development does not solely apply to Francophones: all of Ontarian society, all sectors of its economy, benefit from it.

When we train a doctor in French in Ontario, we also train a doctor capable of treating patients in English and capable of treating patients from minority or immigrant communities. When Ontario subsidizes training in French for a lawyer, the entire society benefits from a lawyer with skills in both languages and in support of minority communities. When Ontario invests in apprenticeship in French for trades such as that of an auto mechanic, this mechanic provides services in French and in English in large automobile companies.

The doctor, lawyer or mechanic is thus committed to his or her life environment, participating in social, sports or cultural activities in French. Not only do they become economic actors, they also fulfil themselves on the human plane. They contribute to social harmony and cohesion thanks to their acquired knowledge and know-how, which they will be able to transmit to other members of their community.

A 2008 report by the Ontario Public Service focused on the theme of diversity. Because a diverse organization is better able to recruit the best talent from a diverse population, it fosters new ideas for improving services and responding to the needs of many different communities. The report identified Francophones as one of the groups targeted for larger representation and recognition in the Ontario Public Service.

The presence of a Francophone community supported by sustainable systemic measures confers upon Ontario a particular status within the Canadian confederation. The province thus participates in the great public debates surrounding Canadian language and culture. In that area, Ontario intends to be an indicator for change, even more so since it is committed on the international stage, alongside 55 countries and States from the Francophonie.

The transition towards sustainable human development in Ontario is a powerful message to minority communities around the world. Education, training and learning become essential human development tools to protect and promote the community.

Indeed, sustainable learning allows the transformation of a demographically marginalized group into a significant socio-economic entity that will adhere to the larger economic and social objectives of the majority community.

This transition supports two conditions for sustainable human development: social harmony and fair distribution of wealth.

I would add that Ontario is continuously facing challenges to ensure sustainable human development for Francophones, specifically: challenges on the demographic plane, the integration of Francophone newcomers, improving health determinants, as well as mobilizing Francophone youth. In this respect, the Government has announced the implementation of a strategy targeting youth and aiming at reinforcing their sense of belonging to the Francophonie within the Ontarian multicultural context.

7

Sustainability and Competitiveness

JEAN LEMIERRE
Former President of the European Bank for
Reconstruction and Development (EBRD)

Sustainability is one of the most difficult subjects to deal with. It is also an extremely timely topic, and one that makes me think back to my adolescence during the 1970s. I remember the Club of Rome and the idea, widely held at the time, that the economy was growing far too quickly and that we had to stop wasting resources. The proposed solution was to return to zero growth.

I have always believed this to be wrong. That was what I thought in the 1970s and it is what I still think today.

It is indisputable that the growth of the world's population and, happily, the improving living standards of a good part of the world—although, unfortunately, far too many people still live in extreme poverty—create a problem of increased demand for natural resources. At the same time, this does not really encourage us to champion the reduction of growth. So, if one cannot stop growth, one must ponder the stakes that concern our entire planet: competitiveness and sustainability, both for businesses and for each and every one of us. And these two ideas, I believe, are not incompatible, in fact quite the contrary.

Many examples can be used to illustrate the fact that, for a business or a community, defending sustainability and maintaining competitiveness are two parts of the same battle. Most large corporations will tell you, and justifiably so, that they are already doing this and managing it quite well; then again, there are also a great many examples to the contrary.

The increase in the price of energy, among other things, is one obvious counter-example. Here the rise in the price of a product, which normally helps to manage scarcity, can have the counter-effect of encouraging the destruction of the environment. We see today—and Canada knows this better than any other country—that new regions are being opened up to oil prospecting, especially in the Arctic. No one would have dreamed of doing this only ten years ago because market prices did not permit it. This is a fundamental dilemma and a serious matter for debate: between obtaining energy supplies and protecting the environment, where should we go? How far can we go?

Let us take a second example, this time from the food sector: GMOs. In order to answer the world's exponentially growing demand for agro-food products, must we energetically commit ourselves to the creation of genetically modified food products or not? Once again, this is an extraordinarily difficult debate with regard to both competitiveness and sustainability and especially with regard to sustainability in matters of health. For health is at the heart of sustainability.

The present situation is characterized by a profound questioning of our way of life. Despite having massive energy needs to meet, we cannot continue to consume energy at the present rate, nor can we emit as much CO_2, or drill everywhere at an accelerating pace.

"Fairness Over Time"

The first point I would like to discuss concerns one of the fundamental principles of sustainability and competitiveness: essentially, to make the best deal possible. And the best long-term deal is not necessarily the best short-term deal. In business management and in the way that markets evaluate their potential return, there is one issue that all parties should consider. This is, to use an English expression that is not especially economic in nature: "fairness over time." What ensures that a petroleum contract will remain fair over time? This is a difficult question to answer. Nonetheless, one can assert that unless the investment has legitimacy, there can be no sustainability. This search for legitimacy rests partly on the economic return and partly on the acceptability of the long-term horizons of investment. This legitimacy represents a cost to businesses. It can mean deferred profits that can have a significant impact on the economic stability of a corporation; however, in the end it is the only way to ensure sustainability. How then, are we to structure long-term investments so as to allow each party to realize a fair portion of both the investment and the profits? Once again, this is an extremely difficult question to answer, but it is of crucial importance.

This is the subject of the debate surrounding infrastructure, especially with regard to setting fair tariffs. And we know very well that if tariffs are not fair and acceptable to all of the various parties *over time*, there is a significant risk that the investment will be lost, or that the infrastructure will be nationalized, or that the investment will not be well maintained.

So sustainability is best achieved by taking greater notice of the long-term aspects of one's investment, in partnership with the communities, countries and municipalities in which the investment is being made. I will not go into details. I could, unfortunately, provide some very unhappy examples of major corporations that were forced to conduct renegotiations—often very difficult renegotiations—because they failed to establish an appropriate division of wealth at the outset.

THE HUMAN ASPECT OF SUSTAINABILITY

There is a second feature as well that is of extreme importance, and this concerns sustainability with regard to the human dimension. I am struck, in most of the large emerging countries, by the lack of attention given to questions of work safety. It is unacceptable to imagine growth that is obtained at the expense of the people of these countries. The problems of mining and traffic accidents are crucial questions that must be dealt with in a framework of investment that is both durable and sustainable. Once again, investment and competitiveness cannot go against human considerations. In countries such as Ukraine, Kazakhstan or Russia, this is an extraordinarily difficult and extremely serious subject. Why? Because we are in the process of using or exploiting certain mineral resources to the maximum extent possible. Therefore, safety problems will definitely increase over time.

The environment is also, without doubt, a concern of the greatest importance. Here too, one can find ways of managing the investment while respecting the environment. The vast majority of very large energy projects raise alarming questions with regard to the environment that cannot be ignored. We cannot accept that short-term profit should be created to the detriment of the environment. I am not saying that we should do this because of the environment, but rather that it is in the interest of the investor to do it. Even though much progress remains to be made concerning this question, this should be achievable.

I would like to mention another aspect of sustainability: beyond investment in matters of safety there is investment in individuals. This concerns education, health, and the promotion of women's rights. The potential of far too many countries today is still not being fully realized, and this is especially true in the large emerging economies.

The Bank did a survey of nearly 30,000 people in Eastern Europe. The goal was to learn what these people thought and hoped for. Two things became extremely clear: for these people, education and health were far more important than democracy. We see a middle class being created in these countries, although one with relatively low income. I am not speaking about oligarchs here, but about this new middle class that we have been hoping to see emerge for the last 15 years. Their aspirations are simple: to have access to work, education and health services for their children.

Here we see the need for the public authorities, in partnership with the private sector this time, to invest very large sums of money in health and education—far more than they are investing today. Here we are less concerned with competitiveness at the level of individual corporations and more on the scale of public systems. In Eastern European countries in particular, a large part of the revenues drawn from the exploitation of oil and gas resources, and other raw materials, must be invested in education and, to a much greater extent than at present, in health. If this is not done, the system will not be sustainable.

The Principle of Precaution

The second-last point I would briefly like to make concerning sustainability and competitiveness is the principle of precaution. I bring it up at this point because the principle of precaution raises, at the same time, both human and scientific concerns. Earlier, I mentioned GMOs. I could also mention investment in the nuclear sector. I think that we must work in a far more transparent manner, holding clear debates on questions such as GMOs and nuclear power, so that the stakes and the risks are perfectly understood, not only by businesses, but also by the communities involved. It is essential that these debates, in all countries, be much more open.

For Better State and Corporate Governance and Greater Transparency

What conclusions can one draw from all this? I am at one and the same time confident and assailed by many questions. I am extremely confident that we can meet the challenge of reconciling sustainable development and competitiveness by employing good management, technology, wise investment and the accountability of governments and businesses as well as individual reponsibility—as long as everyone involved understands the real stakes. And here some extremely relevant questions present themselves, such as the roles of multilateral institutions, regulatory frameworks and national regulatory agencies. Value can only be created within clear frameworks, demarcated by clear legal systems that produce effective legal decisions, so that both short-term and long-term considerations can be taken into account. And the role of the State—not the prescriptive State but the regulatory State—is a role of the highest importance. The State must ensure that the various terms of investment are duly met in order to ensure the creation of value.

Most of the people I speak to in Eastern Europe feel that the West has just destroyed huge amounts of value in the financial markets, and raised the cost of financing their own investments. Equally, they reproach the fact that the western economies have not acted in a sustainable manner, but focused instead on short-term profits. This is a subject on which we should all reflect because it is a question that they have thrown back at us for the first time.

I was very much involved in resolving the financial crisis of 1997-1998. At that time the countries of Eastern Europe were the source of the crisis. Today they have a deep sense that it is we who have created the problem. They say, "But where is your sustainability? Where is your governance? Where are your rules?"

Whereas the markets were extremely liquid until last year and funded all kinds of investments lavishly, today credit is tight. Why this destruction of value? How have we come to this? Quite simply, all this means that we must treat this question firmly, humbly and pragmatically, going step by step, and creating, from this time forward, systems that are less hermetic and far more open.

I believe that there is another extremely important dimension to the idea of competitiveness tied to sustainability, one which I will address in a few closing words. This is a fundamental question and it forces us to pause and reflect. I am referring to the corruption that reigns in certain countries. Corruption is often an obstacle to sustainability and competitiveness. It limits and sets conditions on access to markets, resources and raw materials. It is a destructive phenomenon that greatly undermines everyone's prospects in the countries involved, and leads to the misallocation of resources and capital. It has extremely negative repercussions. The only way to deal with this question is in an honest manner, one that is open, clear and transparent, and does not attempt to bend the normal rules of the marketplace by acting in ways that will inevitably distort competitiveness to the detriment of sustainability.

8

Ecological Measures: Industrial Success

ANDREW FERRIER
Chief Executive Officer of Fonterra, New Zealand

Can competitiveness be reconciled with sustainability? For my company, it has to.

Fonterra is a dairy co-operative, owned by some 10,000 shareholder/suppliers. It is New Zealand's largest dairy co-operative, representing 97% of dairy production and is also New Zealand's largest company with 2007/08 revenues of about US$13.5 billion. Fonterra represents 20% of New Zealand's exports and about 7% of its GDP. Although New Zealand only accounts for 4% of global dairy production, it is unique because it exports 95% of that production. That makes the co-operative Fonterra the largest dairy exporter in the world.

In addition to its New Zealand base, Fonterra also produces dairy products in Australia, China, the United States and South America for international markets. It is truly a global business with core dairy ingredients such as milk powders, butter, cheese and cream comprising two-thirds of revenues, bought by customers in 140 countries. Fonterra's branded consumer products, such as Anchor butter, milk powders and cheese are sold in about 40 countries, particularly in Australasia, Asia, the Middle East, and South and Central America.

Increasingly, Fonterra's customers want to know that it operates a sustainable business, because consumers are increasingly questioning where their food comes from and how it is produced. That concern is extending to the ingredients in manufactured food, and therefore manufacturers must look to their suppliers for evidence of the best practices.

THE ECOLOGICAL IMPACT

Although the necessity to prove that Fonterra's dairy products are produced through sustainable farming and manufacturing processes is not significant yet, it is becoming more important.

Consumers at large, and more specifically Fonterra's customers, are not the only ones putting on the pressure. New Zealand ratified the Kyoto Protocol in 2002, a commitment to reducing greenhouse gas emissions to 1990 levels steadily by 2012. New Zealand is unique because agriculture accounts for nearly 50% of emissions, compared to 7% in most other developed countries. Yet, in just five years it will be the first country in the world to bring agriculture within an emissions trading scheme.

New Zealand has no agricultural subsidies. It is thousands of kilometres away from most of its major customers. So, sustainability and competitiveness have to go hand in hand at Fonterra. The company must be both low cost and top quality, and be able to prove to customers and consumers that it operates in a sustainable way. The priority is very clear—to be the lowest-cost, sustainable dairy company in the world.

In pursuit of that strategy, Fonterra is reducing its ecological impact right across the supply chain, from cow to consumer, and doing it in a way that makes economic sense.

Changing consumer attitudes can succeed in changing producer attitudes. Six years ago, Fonterra was under fierce criticism from shareholders for signing an accord with central and local governments to improve water quality in streams, rivers and lakes. The shareholders assumed at first that would mean higher on-farm costs, because the accord required farm waterways to be fenced to prevent animals from polluting them and bridges provided at crossing points in streams, again to ensure dairy herds are not fouling waterways. However, when the shareholders understood the wider market implications, they moved from critics to converts. Today 83% of dairy cattle are excluded from streams, 97% of farm waterways have bridges or culverts and 97% of farmers are using nutrient budgeting systems to prevent the loss of nutrients such as fertilizers, from farms into waterways.

A measure of those changed attitudes is the supplier/shareholder acceptance of tough environmental performance standards that Fonterra introduced in 2007. The company has made it plain to shareholders that suppliers who fail to meet regulatory standards will incur penalties. Persistent breaches will lead to the ultimate sanction of Fonterra's refusing to collect their milk. The co-operative is targeting a very small minority with these tough sanctions, all with the full support of our responsible shareholders.

However, Fonterra is not reducing its ecological impact simply to earn green credentials with consumers and customers. Everything has to make economic, as well as environmental, sense. There are real triple bottom-line benefits in driving down the consumption of resources, such as energy and water, in reducing our total carbon footprint and in recycling. Just as importantly, operating sustainably earns Fonterra the right to operate in an environmentally conscious country like New Zealand and keeps the company on the right side of regulators wanting to sharpen New Zealand's green credentials through tougher performance standards.

INNOVATION IS A KEY ELEMENT TO SUSTAINABILITY

Innovation plays a critical role in living and working sustainably. It has to, because the current science puts very few useful tools in the hands of farmers when it comes to reducing the greenhouse gas emissions from pastoral farming, something which is so important to meeting New Zealand's Kyoto commitments. Fonterra is turning to innovation to change that.

Fonterra is undertaking research into pastoral genomics to reduce agriculture emissions of greenhouse gases. These mainly originate from fermentation and digestion of forage in the rumen of cows.

The company is a member of the Pastoral Greenhouse Gas Research Consortium, which has invested $15 million to date in ruminant emissions research. The research carried out thus far has significantly advanced the understanding of rumen dynamics and this knowledge forms the essential foundation for the development and testing of potential mitigation tools. The consortium is recognized as a world leader in the field. Another $25 million will be invested over the next five years.

This is a work-in-progress, but the research team has had a breakthrough. They have closed the genome sequence of a methane-forming microbe in cattle and sheep rumen. It is the first rumen methanogen genome to be sequenced in the world and, while it is just one part of the puzzle, it is a milestone in identifying new genes and proteins to inhibit methanogens without affecting productivity.

Right across Fonterra, projects that make both economic and ecological sense are reducing the company's carbon footprint—and reducing costs.

Take energy for example. The company processes 14 billion litres of milk a year at 26 New Zealand sites. Energy is the second highest cost after wages. Every kilowatt saved improves cost structures, while reducing emissions. We began an energy reduction project about four years ago and we have achieved an annual run rate in energy savings of 2.8 petajoules of energy—the equivalent annual energy use of a city of about 260,000 people. This achievement not only makes environmental sense, it makes financial sense.

The payoff for the environment is a 150,000-tonne reduction in CO_2 emissions. Fonterra's energy consumption, per unit of production, has fallen by 10% and we are targeting another 9% reduction. Fonterra's energy reduction program is the largest undertaken by a New Zealand company. In 2005/06 it accounted for 82% of the New Zealand business' total energy savings.

Two years ago, we also set up a simulated emissions trading system in our manufacturing sites. The Carbon Account puts a dollar value on each site's quarterly emissions and it is a powerful tool for driving savings. Since 1990 our manufacturing business has reduced its carbon dioxide emissions per tonne by 28% despite the energy intensity of some new products that are 30% higher than those produced in 1990.

Fonterra has introduced milk concentration technology to reduce tanker movements from farms to factories. We have reprogrammed the national supply chain, moving from trucks to rail, reducing truck movements by more than 45,000 per year, thereby saving a lot of fuel.

Fonterra spends about US$300 million a year on packaging. Again, we focus on environmental and economic payback. Recycling used plastics has almost halved waste costs and Fonterra is well on the way to achieving a 90% reduction in waste to landfill. The company also has redesigned packaging to reduce the use of plastics and paper, an initiative that is good for the environment and good for costs.

A Positive Carbon Footprint

Peer reviewed research by Lincoln University in New Zealand has shown that the New Zealand dairy industry— even with its distance from its markets—is 30% more efficient than its U.K. equivalent in terms of energy and greenhouse gas emissions for products delivered to the U.K.

That is good, but not good enough for Fonterra. It is important to ensure real objectivity in the measurement of an overall carbon footprint. In 2007 Fonterra initiated a massive project to measure its cow-to-consumer carbon footprint, using what we expect will be universally accepted, auditable, standards of measurement.

Fonterra has a complicated supply chain, and it has three research areas: on-farm; processing; and the supply chain to markets.

1. The system boundary for the on-farm module is the farm gate. The unit of measure is per kilogram of total milk solids. Within this module, we are measuring or estimating:

- On-farm pasture production (methane and nitrous oxide from animals);

- Cow management (diesel and gasoline), milk extraction, effluent management and water supply electricity;
- Production of supplementary feed;
- Off-farm dairy replacements; and
- Production and delivery of crop and pasture inputs such as fertilizers, lime, pesticides and seeds.

Fonterra is assessing a wide range of dairy-farm types, comparing organic and conventional farms, and high-producing farms using large quantities of supplementary feed and irrigation systems.

2. For the processing module of research, the key factors are: energy inputs, chemical use, water use, ingredients other than milk to manufacture products, packaging and refrigerants.

The matters we must consider include:

- Best method for calculating the weighted average of our 26 manufacturing plants, each of which produces a range of products;
- Domestic transport logistics; and
- The allocation procedure—noting that many plants produce more than one product.

3. Module three covers the transport of products from warehouse to port, container-vessel fuel and refrigerants, off-loading and repackaging in places like Singapore and transport to the warehouse at the final destination. The calculation finishes at the point where we no longer have ownership of the product or ingredient.

This work will do more than measure our footprint. It will indicate where we can focus to reduce it, while giving us hard data around the gains that we are making through the current environmental initiatives. It is another example of Fonterra's commitment to sustainability.

SUSTAINABILITY AND FOOD SAFETY: CONTRADICTORY NOTIONS?

One of the questions to be addressed is whether the precautionary principle is a drag on innovation. When it comes to food safety, it is critical that Fonterra's products pass all tests in assuring the safety of our food for human consumption: if there is any doubt, the product is not sold. The company institutes rigorous testing of all new products before putting them on the supermarket shelf.

Fonterra is also increasingly applying this principle to the work safety of our manufacturing sites—and we have more than 50 worldwide. The mantra is clear: if there is any doubt about the safety of a piece of equipment, it must be shut down. There is a lot of education to do, but there has been progress.

Food is a major issue. The world has seen prices rise, stockpiles fall, consumers rioting, governments scrambling to keep food within borders by applying export taxes and governments breaking down import barriers to feed their people.

Demand is high and getting higher as a massive middle class emerges in the world and oil-rich countries get richer on the back of the boom. The Food and Agriculture Organization of the United Nations estimates food production will need to double by 2050 to meet demand and ensure food security.

Global production systems are going to come under increasing pressure and with them, the environment. How then will we reconcile economic and environmental sustainability? Will the competitive advantage now held by environmentally conscious producers pass on to those who are the cheapest producers? Will green principles be put aside for political pragmatism, especially in poorer countries?

Fonterra always will see the benefits of environmental sustainability. The company will be faced with lower-cost, less sustainable models, but by keeping to the high road, we firmly believe that we will win in the end.

9

Education and Training in Relation to the Environment: Creating a Dynamic of Social Resilience

LUCIE SAUVÉ, PH.D.
Holder of the Canada Research Chair in Environmental Education
Université du Québec à Montréal (UQAM)

Let us consider education from a global perspective, through the full scope of lifelong education as a process, one that strives to shape a citizenry that is both creative as well as socially and ecologically responsible. Clearly, from this perspective, education in post-secondary institutions and in the workplace must play a major role in promoting social resilience, the capacity to adapt and to transform ourselves as a society as we encounter the turbulence and trials of our rapidly changing world.

Education, then, should not be limited to teaching closed systems of knowledge and specialized know-how and techniques. When acquiring the knowledge of special disciplines and specific professional qualifications, it is also vital to stimulate critical thinking and encourage the growth of creativity. These two abilities work together to prevent our getting stuck in the rut of short-term solutions. They open up new horizons of knowledge and lead us toward a better way of "Living together on Earth."[1] The goal here is to live a better life together as human beings from different societies, and as living beings amidst other life forms and life systems in their supportive environments of which we are integral parts.

Technological Innovation and Development: Yes, But Then What?

Clearly, technological innovation and development have important roles to play in encouraging socio-ecological viability. For example, the capture of energy from high-altitude winds, the manufacture of bio-fuels from waste material, or the storage of solar energy: all are highly promising developments.[2] Nevertheless, this is not enough.

It is increasingly admitted that change, the necessary transition to the future, requires our ability to reinvent the very meaning of our world. This will come about, among other means, by a careful deconstruction of the foundation and structure of power, great and small, in our society. For power in our society, as we all well know, is oriented toward the accumulation of short-term profit that benefits only the few individuals who have appropriated one type of market economy. Take the example of the recent General Motors plant closings. The suffering this has caused clearly demonstrates that short-term economic goals only lead to a dead end and encourage unsustainable social values. Consider, for a moment, the fact that the scarcity of petroleum has been well known for over half a century and climate change has been predicted for

---

1. "Living together on Earth" is the theme of the 5th World Environmental Education Congress, Montreal, May 10-14, 2009: www.5weec.uqam.ca
2. The magazine *Discover* published a special anniversary issue (October 2008): "67 Ways to reinvent the world."

decades. Our society has, however, ignored these warnings, blinded by the flow of short-term profits.

The greatest challenge facing many industries today—such as tobacco, lumber, pork and waste management, to name just a few—is not, as one might imagine, that of holding on for as long as possible with the help of government subsidies and technological acrobatics. Rather it is the challenge of reinventing themselves in order to respond as adequately as possible and in the most socially and ecologically responsible way possible to our society's basic needs for food, health, transportation, housing, leisure, etc. In their present form, these industries are in fact headed for oblivion.

For businesses, as for individuals, complete self-transformation requires appropriate training. It calls first for an initial education that is both general and specialized. Then it requires ongoing training that becomes, in time, a self-reflective approach and a permanent part of the company's functioning. This process also requires a commitment to society as a whole, for 'no business is an island, complete unto itself.' Every business is an open system in constant interaction with the society around it.

STIMULATING INNOVATION TO CREATE MAJOR SOCIAL CHANGE: THE CHALLENGE THAT TRAINING MUST MEET

Social and technological innovation must be envisioned in terms of a profound change in the relational dynamics between individuals, social groups and the environment. Technological "Band-Aid solutions" have proved to be costly and temporary. For example, all too often the relentless pursuit of progress in the field of agricultural biotechnology merely puts off and, in the long run, amplifies problems that are already well known in intensive agriculture. Innovation calls for the exercise of a critical and acute outlook that grasps realities beyond the short and medium term, and one that stimulates useful alternative approaches.

The development of this critical competence[3] must integrate three kinds of knowledge. First, a range of general and specialized knowledge that allows one to consider the facts from different angles and in different ways. Critical thinking does not occur in a vacuum: it requires content, cultural context and points of reference. Secondly, critical competence requires cognitive ability—analysis, synthesis, evaluation, etc.—and strategic abilities, such as those needed for research, information processing, developing an argument or debate, etc. Thirdly, it calls for certain attitudes—scepticism, curiosity, the capacity to question things—and for certain values, notably rigour and the concern for relevance and accuracy. All these encourage a critical approach to reality. Thus, mastering critical competence means knowing how to exercise critical thinking in a pertinent and effective way within a specific context.[4]

There are endless objects and circumstances upon which to exercise critical thought. Some examples: one can assess the advantages and limitations of a public policy concerning the environment; determine the biases and weaknesses of a documentary on climate change; identify the elements that aim at

---

3. These ideas are more extensively explained and elaborated in the following editorial article: Sauvé, L. and Orellana, I. (2008). "Conjuguer rigueur, équité, créativité et amour: L'exigence de la criticité en éducation relative à l'environnement." *Éducation relative à l'environnement – Regards, Recherches, Réflexions,* Volume 7, pp. 7-23.
4. Guy Le Boterf clarifies the notion of competence in general. To the three sorts of knowledge usually mentioned as aspects of competence, he adds the desire to act and the ability to act: Le Boterf, G., *Construire les compétences individuelles et collectives : Agir et réussir avec compétence,* 4th edition, Paris: Éditions Organisations, 2006.

improving an urban development plan; participate effectively in public debates on environmental questions; and evaluate the relevance and internal coherence of an eco-development project.

All the same, reflecting on the "what" and the "how" of the matter are not enough. The essential critical question is "why." Coherent critical competence requires a critical spirit concerning society. Who decides what and why? In whose name and to what end, or to exercise what power? It is from such a perspective that socio-ecological questions must be raised. The same is true of questions concerning energy and water.

Equally, this social critical perspective must be self-reflective: Who are we? Where and how do we live? What do we want to do? What can we do collectively? How wide is our freedom of action? What are the barriers to realizing our goals? Where and with which tools can power be exerted?

Beyond the deconstruction of social realities, this kind of questioning opens new horizons of transformation and reconstruction. For example, in environmental matters, would not the most urgent and least costly course of action in the short run be that of using and optimizing so-called "appropriate" technologies? These simple and proven technologies are the result of past experience, and have been adapted to their environments. Similarly, would not the most urgent thing simply be, in many cases, to apply existing laws and regulations, giving us an efficient means of control?

Teaching and learning to practice 'critical thinking' means being grounded in logic, clarity and coherence, and it involves the search for what is "true" amid the fog of the "false." Yet we can go beyond this, enriching education by communicating the foundation and practices of what is called "critical pedagogy."

"Critical pedagogy" is concerned with social values: justice, equality, solidarity, democracy and collective emancipation. We are concerned here with belief systems and societal mechanisms that reinforce certain powers and, also, with power structures in society that determine what is possible and what is not and that favour certain social groups over others.[5] We would like to call the public's attention to the following: the way that critical thought is used is itself often influenced by power games. These power games in turn bear the mark of frames of reference that influence analysis and critical judgment.

One must also note that teachers of critical thinking do not see it as an exclusively intellectual activity that is remote from action. Theory and practice overlap each other, mutually transforming and illuminating each other, creating meaning and transformative knowledge. The question then, is not "how to do it?" but rather "why do it?" and also, "could we do something different and do it differently?" In critical pedagogy, the significance of different realities is of prime importance. The critical posture requires the individual to fully commit himself to act in a fully coherent manner, as indicated by Joe L. Kincleloe (2005) in his work *Critical Pedagogy*.[6]

AND AS TO SUSTAINABLE DEVELOPMENT?

Such pedagogical preoccupations lead us to critically confront the concept of sustainable development itself, which is usually presented as a pillar of a new social correctness. What

5. These ideas are developed in the following text, in Burbule, N.C. and Berk, R. (1991): "Critical Thinking and Critical Pedagogy: Relations, Differences and Limits," in Popkewitz, T.S. and Fendler, L. *Critical Theories in Education: Changing Terrains of Knowledge and Politics* (pp. 45-65). NY: Routledge.
6. Kincheloe, J.L., *Critical Pedagogy. Primer.* New York: Peter Lang, 2005.

is its origin? Why has the ideology of sustainable development exercised such a powerful attraction and become so influential today? What needs, what anxieties and what social experiences does it attempt to answer and fulfil? What vision of the world underlies this ideology of sustainable development?

Here the economy is generally presented as an exogenous entity, peripheral to society, one that imposes its own rules on the relationship between society and the environment, a nameless, faceless economy, devoid of social responsibilities, since it is outside the social sphere. It might well be described as "desocialized." Thus, the environment is reduced to the sum of resources available for economic development. Nature and life have no other meaning than that defined through development. One agrees not to exceed the capacity of the eco systems, not for their own sakes: rather, it is to prevent any disruption of economic development.

Society, in such a context, defines itself as consisting of producers and consumers, of human resources and beneficiaries or clients in the service of economic development. So we read in a recent report published by the United Nations that "sustainable development depends on maintaining adequate supplies of capital: financial, manufactured, natural, human and social capital."[7] This logic saturates the proposed subject matter concerning "education in the light of sustainable development" as outlined in another report published by the OECD.[8] It proposes the integration into the curricula of all schools—from elementary schools to university—of subject

7. United Nations (2008). *Measuring Sustainable Development*. On line: http://www.oecd.org/topic/0,3373,fr_2649_37425_1_1_1_1_37425,00.html, document consulted in October 2008.
8. OECD (2008). *Report on OECD Workshop on Education for Sustainable Development*, Paris, October 2008, p. 7. On line: http://www.oecd.org/topic/0,3373,fr_2649_37425_1_1_1_1_37425,00.html, document consulted in October 2008.

matter for teaching and training that is essentially economic in nature, or defined against economic criteria and presented from the perspective of growth.[9]

Does this vision of the world really suit us, a vision put forward by the politico-economic authorities of the world, as the basis for a worldwide educational program? Can we really be happy in the long term with a sustainable development compromise, however tempting and persuasively promised it might be?[10] How can one avoid the excesses that this concept has so often permitted?[11] What other visions of the world could be imagined? Research, reflection and practice in the fields of political ecology, social ecology, eco-development and eco-feminism, among others, present us with a whole range of alternatives that must be explored. Each in their own way, within the context of their own social group, can pursue their own "invention of the world" founded upon a "new narrative of the world," to use the apt expression coined by Riccardo Petrella, the political scientist, economist and founder of the Lisbon Group and the International Committee for the World Water Contract.[12]

---

9. Christian Laval and Louis Weber analyze this kind of proposition coming from international organizations: Laval, C. and Weber, L. (2002). *Le nouvel ordre éducatif mondial.* Paris: Éditions Nouveaux Regards et Éditions Syllepse.

10. Many authors—philosophers, sociologists, economists, political scientists, educators, agronomists, etc.—have contributed to the critique of "sustainable development." Let us mention, among others, Gilbert Rist (1996) and Serge Latouche (2004). Their analyses converge: "sustainable development" is a far too narrowly defined frame of reference (indeed, a deforming one) with which to create a social project and even less an educational project: Latouche, S. (2004). *Survivre au développement,* Coll. Les Petits Livres. No 55. Paris: Mille et une nuits; Rist, G. (1996). *Le développement, Histoire d'une croyance occidentale,* Paris: Sciences Po.

11. The authors of the following article explain some of the stakes of "sustainability" as a theme running through higher education, in Wals, A.E.J. and B. Jickling, 2002: "Sustainability in Higher Education: From doublethink and newspeak to critical thinking and meaningful learning." *International Journal of Sustainability in Higher Education.* 3(3): p. 221-232.

12. Petrella, R., *Pour une nouvelle narration du monde.* Montréal: Écosociété, 2007.

This is where creativity intervenes. The exercise of "criticality" (critical thought in conjunction with social critique) can offer an extraordinary springboard for creativity. Beyond the work of deconstruction, one must envisage reconstruction. In environmental matters, creativity should preferably be a collective activity wherein the dynamics of discussion, exchange and collaborative work stimulate the emergence of new ideas and allow them to be tested and improved. The creative process has not been well enough documented. Too often we fail to celebrate the courageous, humble and smaller-scale initiatives that, little by little, allow crucial fundamental change to begin.

How Can Post-Secondary and Corporate Education Contribute to the Development of Eco-Citizenship?

First, as we have already briefly indicated, the initial training in educational establishments must not focus solely on the transmission of specific competencies. It should invest the student with a broad culture, especially with regard to the environment and society. This culture is indispensable if the student is to think critically and creatively. One's main education is enriched by a critical knowledge of various ways to conceive and do things, including alternative paths that can bring about positive change.

We can identify four main paths toward the integration of environmental education and training into establishments of higher learning (colleges, universities, institutes, etc.). The paths are complementary and overlap each other:

The "ecologization" of infrastructure— architecture, planning, resource management— and lifestyles within the institution

It is vital to recognize the importance of a "pedagogy of place"[13] and to implement it: walls, devices and daily practices all "speak." More than long speeches, they transmit an institutional message: that concern for the environment and for the well-being of other people is important. This is expressed in the ways resources are used in offices, classrooms, laboratories, cafeterias, etc., and also in the way people interact with each other and with their surroundings. All this testifies to a culture of ecology.

The "ecologization" of training programs

This involves incorporating an environmental dimension into the courses of the different disciplines: biology, chemistry, social sciences, management science, philosophy, arts, design, etc. Each discipline must be concerned with the relationship to the environment of its subject matter and its practices. But it is equally vital to create interdisciplinary opportunities and other means of cross-fertilized learning that will permit a global approach to the realities of our world. Finally, we must firmly set the context of training within the realities of life environments in order to give greater meaning and relevance to the learning process. The critical exploration of oneself and one's milieu in relation to this milieu (one's college, neighbourhood, city, region) becomes a vital starting point and a framework for an educational program in relation to the environment.

---

13. David Orr has widely promoted the ecologization of campuses: Orr, D. *Ecological Literacy – Education and the transition to a postmodern World.* Albany: State University of New York Press, 1992.

Since our modern lives are characterized by mobility, we must learn to root ourselves in the here and now, in the midst of our communities, for this is the only space-time that is given to us to inhabit, now and forever. This is our only encounter with life, with nature and the environment, our only encounter with reality. Our connection with the environment can only exist in this context; it must be embodied and experienced in this place that we inhabit — be it ever so briefly — rather than "possess." The experience, moreover, of being 'anchored' in a specific context can be transferred elsewhere: it is, fundamentally, a question of developing our capacity to root ourselves amidst the life systems and living beings that surround us, *wherever we may be.*

Directing research towards socio-ecological matters of concern

We have increasingly come to value interdisciplinary and participatory research that allows us to deal with complex problems in a global way. Partnerships between the various sectors of institutional research and involvement in the community or the corporate context are strongly encouraged. Equally, we have come to recognize the close ties between research and training, the enrichment of training by research and the potential for research projects to provide a context for training students. Thus enlightened by a critical approach, research can become a powerful driver for social and technological innovation. It can inspire needed changes of direction as to the fundamental choices facing our societies. We are now concerning ourselves with the social utility of research and the social responsibility of the researcher, a responsibility that must go far beyond the deontology of science today.

Serving the world's communities by means of training programs, international co-operation projects and other means

These are contexts in which the citizen can take part in solving socio-ecological problems. In this regard, I recall the initiative taken by the vice-rector of the University of Veracruz who, with the collaboration of some of the students, set up a social services centre in one of the poorer neighbourhoods of the city. It became a training centre for future dentists, nurses, nutritionists, social workers, forest managers, managers, biologists and educators, among others, all of whom found it to be a favourable context within which to take a multidisciplinary approach to socio-ecological realities.

As the work of Peter Blaze Corcoran and Arjen Wals demonstrates,[14] the integration of an environmental dimension into schools of higher learning has been encouraged until now by a number of declarations and programs created by international organizations, especially UNESCO. Over time, the process has been enriched by the experience of a growing number of institutions committed to an environmental or a sustainable development policy. These institutions, which have innovated in the ecologization of their campuses and curricula, have assumed their socio-ecological responsibility in their milieu.

All the same, there is still much to do before a majority of post-secondary establishments become examples, sources of inspiration and drivers of social change, while fulfilling their traditional mission and with flawless accountability for their public funding.

---

14. Corcoran, P. and Wals, A. (Dir.), *Higher Education and the Challenge of Sustainability - Problematics, Promise, and Practice*, New York: Springer, 2004.

One must, in conclusion, consider corporate training, which has become an integral part of the strategies of eco-responsibility, or "sustainable development," in this area of activity. Unfortunately, little is known about workplace training programs. They are usually offered by consulting firms and their training plans are not generally available for purposes of analysis. They are, to some extent, 'private preserve' and are often concerned only with technological possibilities and management science. To my knowledge, there is little available specialized research literature about these training practices. These firms appear to maintain very few research and development links to the university milieu, even though the trainers usually come from this context. This is, therefore, a research domain to be developed.

However, the corporate training to which I have had access confirms the relevance of the basic principles of andragogy. Initial training that consists only of information transmitted by experts is likely to not make much of a mark. It is better, instead, to have the employees actively engaged in the training process. They can be invited, for example, to take part in an environmental audit or help resolve problems in "their" corporation concerning energy, materials, water use, air quality, workplace quality, etc. Workplace health and safety provides an excellent entry point for involving a company's personnel. It is very often the employees who are best acquainted with the realities of their workplace. It is important to value their experience, their judgment and their creativity, because this acknowledgement is an essential source of motivation and involvement for them. The process of obtaining ISO 14 000 certification, for example, will be much more efficient if the employees are invited to participate. If it is necessary to transform the corporation on an ongoing basis, the contribution of the employees is essential. It is, after all, a matter of their employment security, among other things.

Finally, we see that many companies and institutions offer their employees a range of courses or activities, with the proclaimed purpose of increasing their productivity, such as relaxation sessions and sports or cultural programs. Why not offer activities focused on eco-citizenship, dealing with various aspects of our relationship to the environment and to other people at home, in the garden and in the contexts of transportation, food, health, leisure, etc?

We are dealing here with education, which is something much larger than "training." It aims far beyond the transmission or construction of specific knowledge and know-how. Education is, above all, concerned with the individual as a complete being, in all his or her individual and social dimensions.

Education is concerned with creating what may be called "being-in-the-world." To be in-the-world with others means to share and to see our environment as a home for our communal life—*Oïkos*, from the ancient Greek "home"—a place where we must learn to live together. We must therefore envision an education that is at once ecological, economic and ecosophic. We must learn to find our human "ecological niche" within the entirety of life systems around us and learn to attend to it adequately. We must learn to use communal resources responsibly and interdependently. We must learn to give a sense of meaning to our brief time on earth.

It is within the perspective of such an educational project, carried forward by the different participants in an "educational society," that initial education and ongoing training can contribute to the development of social resilience. They can help us to renew our fundamental ties to the environment and to other living beings—and not just to human beings. They can help us to reinvent our ways of being and of acting, of producing and consuming, through the dual prisms of criticality and creativity.

10

Settling Social Inequalities

DONALD KABERUKA
President of the African Development Bank Group (AfDB)

More than 20 years ago, the World Commission on Environment and Development, known as the Brundtland Commission, first made use of a concept: sustainable development as "meeting the needs of the present without compromising the ability of future generations to meet their own needs."

We are still on notice today in spite of progress and there are daily reminders. This is exemplified by changes in climate that dramatically affect water supplies and exacerbate droughts, by unreliable rain patterns and, as a result, growing poverty in the world and its consequences for millions. In June 2008 the International Community was meeting at a conference in Rome to discuss the food crisis. Among the issues discussed were biofuels and the impact on food security. Twenty-five years after the Brundtland Commission, we are still searching for a consensus on how to reconcile economic development and environmental sustainability. It is the responsibility of the business sector, the public sector, civil society, indeed us all.

Wealth Is Not Well Distributed

We need to go beyond first-level sustainability. Today, to put it simply, 20% of the world's population live in wealthy countries, and they control 85% of the world's wealth. Recent economic advances in emerging countries have led to an increase in the number of people who could be described as rich. But still, this leaves millions in the world surviving on less than the equivalent of two dollars per day, and lacking basic needs. The most vulnerable of these are described as "the bottom billion." The challenge therefore is how to ensure that this "bottom billion"—those who are left out—can converge with the rest of the world. A world of misery side by side with affluence is not sustainable.

Yet, in the experience of emerging countries like China, India and Brazil, countries which are now moving into the league of OECD standards of living, we can see what that transformation process means for sustainability: an increasing pressure on natural resources such as water, soils and forests.

We are told that one of the reasons for the current food crisis is the changing lifestyles among emerging economies. If people eat more beef, there is less grain. And that means, for the bottom billion, less food.

Equity, Justice and Social Equilibrium

No agenda for sustainability can have meaning unless it is founded on equity, justice and social equilibrium between nations, within nations, the stability of our societies and the peaceful coexistence of the world's rich and advanced varied civilizations, all within the context of efforts to preserve the planet and its eco-systems. Failure to do so would have wide consequences globally. As resources become scarce, there are increases in competition for fuel and food, displacement of peoples, regional tensions and unmanageable migratory flows. I am told emerging wealthy countries are drawing on natural resources like farmland, timber and water, twice as fast as those resources can be renewed, with an ecological footprint doubling since the 1960s.

Fighting poverty through economic growth while maintaining the stability of our planet, and transiting to low-carbon economies, are agendas that are part of the larger global discourse on aid, trade and climate change.

While many nations are able to prosper by way of expanding world commerce and development, effective aid is still needed for others. I applaud the efforts of rich countries such as Canada, which are significantly scaling up aid to low-income countries. As Africa's Development Bank our task is to leverage aid money in order to maximize the catalytic effects of private resources. Sustainable development is not possible without creating the conditions for investment. This encourages growth that will sustain people beyond aid and the reason for this is straightforward: people everywhere do not like to be dependent on aid and charity. This is true within countries and between countries. People look for sustainable means to fend for themselves.

At the African Development Bank, we provide support to our countries in order to reduce the risks and costs of doing business, and to expand the scope and depth of Africa's economic integration. We do so by building capable states and strong institutions, through infrastructure, regional integration and promotion of the private sector.

Development, Innovation and Public-Private Partnerships

Poor infrastructure is holding back progress in many areas. In the first few years of Africa's independence, the limited infrastructure was barely enough to support development. Today, as our economies grow at an average of 6%, almost every country on the continent is running short of energy. One of our main challenges now is to develop clean energy from our sizable hydropower potential of which only 4% is developed. Given the paucity of public resources, there is now an opportunity here for the private sector. Now is the time to discuss how Africa can develop its clean energy in public-private sector partnerships.

In the search for sustainable development, innovation remains important and businesses will always be in the forefront. The development and deployment of many of these technologies are beyond the pockets of poor-country governments and will require international cooperation and the private sector.

Let me conclude my remarks by observing that it is only positive interdependence among nations and between nations, governments, civil society, and the private sector that will enable us to make human progress sustainable. It is that interdependence that will enable us to feed the hungry and to foster second-generation biofuels while not diminishing the availability of food. It is those partnerships that will allow poor countries to access technologies that enable adaptation to climate changes, and produce clean energy to fuel the economic growth necessary for poverty eradication—surely the main struggle for mankind in this century.

11

Strategies for Sustainable Development

GÉRARD MESTRALLET
Chairman and CEO of GDF SUEZ

For GDF SUEZ, as for many other companies today, the fundamental challenge is how to reconcile economic development with sustainable development. Can companies be at the same time profitable, responsible and viable in the long term? I am absolutely certain that they can. Companies can and must be responsible, and commit themselves wholeheartedly to the path of sustainable development. Not only is this their obligation towards the societies that permit them to exist, but it is also in their own interest, not only in the long term but also in the short term.

I would like to speak to you today as the head of an enterprise that is active in the fields of energy and the environment, fields that are at the very heart of the problems of sustainable development. But I would also like to speak to you as a citizen of the world who is personally concerned with these questions. I have the honour of heading the French office of the UN Global Compact, a leadership platform which brings over 450 corporations together today in France.

Since its creation, Suez has passed through three great phases of development. In the beginning there was the canal, the standard-bearer of the company, and it remained our focus for more than a century. During the second phase, which lasted almost 40 years, Suez became a banking enterprise with, among others, the Indo-Suez Bank.

Twelve years ago, the Suez Group completely transformed itself and since then has worked in the environmental and energy sectors.

In July 2008, Suez and Gaz de France merged. The GDF SUEZ Group now has an annual turnover of US$100 billion and a capitalization of approximately US$150 billion.

RECONCILING ECONOMIC DEVELOPMENT AND SUSTAINABILITY

In order to succeed, an enterprise such as GDF SUEZ must work with three different time horizons. First there is the short-term horizon of the financial markets. Then that of men and organizations—it sometimes takes a generation to change the culture of a corporation! Then there is the industrial time horizon. Investments in the environment and energy are investments made over lengthy cycles. For a nuclear power station—and GDF SUEZ has seven—the cycle is 60 years; for a dam, it is one hundred years, even two centuries. And ultimately, one must know how to harmonize these three time horizons with Nature and attempt to minimize the ecological footprint we inevitably leave for future generations.

For a corporation, sustainable development is in essence the harmonization of these three different time horizons. One must reconcile the growth, development and social responsibility of the business with the preservation of the environment and the available resources.

I do not believe that one should place finance in opposition to industry, or finance and industry in opposition to ecology. On the contrary, one must attempt to bring them together. I believe this is absolutely essential.

Sustainable development answers three of the core convictions of a group such as GDF SUEZ: to know our business / to provide sustainable solutions to our clients; to assume our responsibilities / to reduce the effects of our activities on the planet; and to realize our vocation / to create wealth that is reliable and sustainable.

Sustainable development is also, and above all, strategic for the Group, for it is a vector of value and performance for our enterprise. In particular it allows our corporate clients to reduce their costs, to increase their competitiveness and productivity through innovation, to develop new markets and to maintain their reputations. For GDF SUEZ it is a means of better anticipating long-term risks. It is the strategic axis of our business and a lever of growth for our activities.

The beginning of the 21st century has been marked by a growing awareness linked to a dilemma. We have realized, fortunately, that economic growth, which until now has been based on the massive exploitation of natural resources, is quite simply no longer viable. The dilemma is that it is equally impossible to abandon the idea of growth. We are no longer in the era of the Club of Rome which, 30 years ago, drew attention to the limits of our resources and put forward the principle of zero growth.

What Transition, Then, Is Possible and How Can We Bring it About?

I believe that we must promote sustainable modes of production, and we must reconsider our habits of consumption. We must reinvent growth and make it ecological; however, this revolution toward sustainable modes of production and sustainable consumption must not be a symptom of negative growth. Indeed, in a world in which three billion people live on less than two euros a day, this concept is simply unthinkable. It would mean making inequality permanent in our world. The necessity of change, therefore, forces us to rethink growth in a world of limited natural resources and of a threatened ecological balance.

The technologies needed to respond to this new paradigm already exist. Progress in this regard will permit us to create sustainable modes of consumption and production. Indeed, the challenge of global warming must not be seen as our inevitable fate, but rather as a catalyst for innovation, and as an opportunity to put in place a new form of ecological growth. All this, however, cannot come about without a profound change in our individual and collective behaviour, both as producers, which we are, but also as consumers, which we are as well.

Six Ideas on One Theme

First idea

There is no one solution, but rather a range of solutions. Therefore, global or supra-regional policy co-ordination is essential. GDF SUEZ, for example, is a partner in the Mediterranean union project, the goal of which is to study practical ways of co-ordinating and acting with regard to water resources, the protection of these resources and access to energy. We have worked on a project concerning the Dead Sea for example, where the goal was to evaluate different ways of preventing its disappearance due to evaporation, which is expected to occur within 20 years if nothing is done. One possibility: one could channel water to it from the Red Sea or the Mediterranean, desalinating some of the water in the process for use by the Palestinians, who need it urgently, while at the same time using the difference of land level—the Dead Sea being the lowest point on the planet, at 400 metres below sea level—to produce enough energy to run the desalination plant.

The technologies for this exist; the problems, however, are not technical—they are essentially political. All the same, we must improve the efficiency of our existing technologies. This does not require as much compromising as one might imagine. The report on climate change by the GIEC—the intergovernmental group of experts working on climate evolution—has shown that the cost of stopping global warming is manageable and much less than the cost of inaction, which will, in fact, be fatal.

Let us take the example of energy efficiency. Today this is, in my opinion, an issue of the greatest importance. Indeed I believe that we have just experienced a third energy shock, to which we have not, perhaps, reacted with as much vigour as we did to the first oil shock in the 1970s. Let us consider, for example, the fact that Moscow uses as much natural gas as the entire country of France. Clearly there are savings that can be realized.

The European Union has set itself the goal of reducing the energy consumption of its member states by approximately

20% by 2020. Energy efficiency should therefore result in a reduction in energy consumption. Moreover, we plan on a significant decrease in pollution and a reduction in cost, all the while maintaining the same quality of service and comfort for our clients. At GDF SUEZ, we believe this is possible.

The goal is to use energy better by focusing on technologies that perform better and by optimizing existing installations. For players in the energy sector, this is a fundamental issue. GDF SUEZ has positioned itself in the market by presenting its clients with an integrated offer of natural gas and electricity along with a range of services designed to reduce CO_2 emissions and energy consumption.

At GDF SUEZ, one of our subsidiary companies will be dedicated exclusively to energy efficiency. It will eventually employ 80,000 people and its annual revenues should grow to US$20 billion.

Our experience with Volvo is another example of concrete action that can be taken. In Belgium, we designed and built for Volvo a world first: the first factory ever in the automobile industry that produces absolutely no CO_2 emissions. The energy used in the plant is entirely renewable: wind, biomass and solar. The CO_2 emissions have gone from 14,000 tonnes in 2004 to zero.

Second idea

We should redefine progress to involve all forms of energy. Here again, there is no single solution, as the various kinds of energy each have their role to play. From 2005 to 2008, almost all forms of fossil fuel saw their prices double. As of now, we know that by 2020-2030, if present trends continue, the demand for energy will go up significantly and fossil fuels will still be almost 80% of our energy sources.

How, in such circumstances, can one guarantee both adequate supplies of energy and national energy security, while remaining competitive? We believe that the answer lies in the *mix* of energy, a balanced combination relying on all forms of energy production: hydroelectricity, nuclear energy, the renewable energy of wind, biomass, and solar, but also gas and even coal.

How can we finance a future without CO_2? The rise in energy prices forces us to invest in the research and development of technological solutions that, in some cases, are not yet commercially viable. This is the case, for example, with CO_2 capture and storage, for which viable technologies and regulatory frameworks are not yet ready for implementation. There is hope however, and there is a definite need for such solutions when we realize that China is building a new coal-fired electrical power plant every day.

One thing is certain: to answer the rising demand for energy, energy specialists have no choice but to increase production capacity while employing the latest technologies to counteract the effects of global warming.

What does this mean for GDF SUEZ? It means increasing our capacity to generate electricity without producing CO_2, primarily by using renewable energy. At GDF SUEZ, 18% of our energy production capacity will be in renewable energy by 2009. Given that the European goal is 20% by 2020, GDF SUEZ will do better, more rapidly, and even go beyond the stated objective.

It will also be vital to participate actively in applied research on carbon capture and storage, and to invest in the research and development of fourth generation nuclear energy.

Already, 40% of our production capacity creates no CO_2 emissions and 40% more creates very little. In France today,

GDF SUEZ's energy production facilities, altogether, do not emit CO_2, thanks to hydraulic, nuclear and wind energy.

Third idea

We have to redefine our relationship to the environment. Climate change has gone beyond being a potential danger and has become a real menace to global ecosystems. Take, for example, water: today only 0.5% of all the water resources on the planet are available for human use and only 2% of treated waste-water is reused. Contrary to the commonly held view, access to potable water does not depend exclusively on the availability of resources. It also depends on the efficient management of these resources, and in this context water resources can, for now, only be managed locally. Here too technical solutions exist, for recycling wastewater and for the desalination of seawater. It is now possible, for example, to recycle wastewater by means of reverse osmosis membranes. It is nevertheless important to use these methods in the most effective way possible and, above all, on a global scale.

Fourth idea

We must profoundly rethink our economic models. As the Secretary-General of the United Nations, Mr. Ban Ki-moon, has stated, it is not just a matter of creating a better world, one that is more healthy and secure for all: it is also about creating a pathway to a major ecological redirection of our world's economy.

In Europe today, new initiatives are emerging that offer a solution. Their goal is to replace the linearity of our economy as we know it, a linearity that moves goods forward in a straight line from the factory where the goods are created, to the delivery point where they are used and thrown away—and all this with no thought given to the depletion of resources. It is essential to move from this linear economy to a circular economy that is focused on eco-industrial development that will reutilize waste materials and used products by recycling them and by maximizing the use of energy.

At GDF SUEZ, for example, we work hard to create partnerships with large industrial corporations in order to recover materials at the end of the economic cycle: cars, planes, boats, household appliances, etc. The materials reclaimed in this way—plastic, metal, glass, etc.—could be recycled and used in the manufacture of new products, or used to produce energy.

Fifth idea

We must think globally but act locally together with the public authorities. Let me stress the importance of obtaining governmental commitment. I believe that it is up to governments to create a context that is favourable to energy savings, to protecting the environment and to sustainable development, so that these concepts are no longer seen as cost generators but, on the contrary, as being profitable for all. All partnerships with the private sector must be based on clear and transparent rules. The public authorities must create the public policies, define the projects and oversee their being carried out. It will be up to the private sector to provide the technical expertise, the know-how and the capacity for innovation. I believe these roles must be clearly defined. And as to the question of how governments and businesses can work together, I would insist on the necessity of creating public-private partnerships.

It may eventually prove wise to combine private funds with national and multilateral funding. That is a political decision. The public authorities should have the initiative and the control—the private sector, the execution and the management. This is how public-private partnerships must be set up. If the rules are clearly defined and consistent over time—with a constancy that should be reaffirmed every time multilateral and supranational authorities can do so—then the private sector, if it reckons it to be worthwhile, if it increases its visibility and if there is a reasonable level of profitability, will invest. I am certain that it will. But once again, the roles must be clearly defined: the public authorities decide, the private sector does the work.

Sixth and last idea

We must rethink the framework of our lives on a large scale. To be a citizen of the world involves both rights and duties: the right to a healthy environment and access to resources, and the duty to respect the rules of our collective existence and to use resources responsibly.

It is up to public authorities to create the means for us to live better together, and it is up to each of us, every citizen, to respect these rules. Europe has taken a lead in creating a detailed action plan concerning questions of climate and energy. The strategies put forward propose a component focused on eco-innovation designed to promote environmental protection and to preserve natural resources, competitiveness and jobs.

But the desire and will for change is beginning to be seen everywhere in the world, as a greater and greater place is being made for green industries, for technologies that respect the climate, for the fight against air pollution, for the management of waste water and for recycling.

New initiatives are seeing the light of day around the world, including in China, a country where the authorities are putting in place a regulatory framework that will promote the creation of eco-parks and eco-cities throughout the country. This ambitious project foresees the creation of 400 brand new ecological cities that should accommodate 300 million people from the countryside by 2020.

I act as a consultant to the mayors of Shanghai and Chongqing and I am struck by the serious concern of China's leaders with regard to these questions. Of course, the demographic stakes in China are very high. Chongqing is the largest city in the world, with more than 33 million inhabitants, more than the population of Canada.

This phenomenon is not unique to China. In Qatar, for example, GDF SUEZ will be acting as a partner to the local authorities in the creation of new cities. An ecological city is one that does not emit CO_2, a city that consumes less energy than it produces, a city that recycles completely, both its waste and the water that it uses. Elsewhere in the Middle East, in China, in India and in other parts of the world, such as Europe, eco-communities are springing up.

I have a deep conviction that the means of achieving this great transformation already exist. They are, in fact, within our grasp. But the real revolution, surely, must be the transformation of our convictions first, and then the transformation of both our habits and our actions.

Living Together in a Globalized World: The Importance of Rethinking our Values and Culture

MICHÈLE S. JEAN
President, Canadian Commission for UNESCO

> *Yes, history is the tragedy of humanity making history, without knowing the history it is making.* (TRANSLATION)
>
> — Raymond Aron

A BACKGROUND OF MULTIPLE PARADOXES

The presentations I attended during the Conference of Montreal described for us, each in their own way, the new avenues—hard but not impossible—that we will have to follow if we are to reconcile innovation, competitiveness and sustainable development. As explained by Jean Lemierre (until recently President of the European Bank for Reconstruction and Development), the good news is that more people in a growing global population are able to buy houses, automobiles and good food; the bad news is that this success partly contributes to the increase in the number of people without the capacity to do so and also has an impact on our capacity to sustain this growth. Another paradox is that economic growth in the 50 least developed countries is the highest in 30 years, but the number of poor continues to rise. In 2005, out of a total population of 767 million, there were 581 million people living on an income of less than the equivalent of two dollars a day. Also, in many countries, the poor spend as much as 70% to 80% of their income on food.[1]

It is worth noting that the gap between rich and poor has also widened in several developed countries during the past ten years, including Canada, according to a report published by the OECD in October 2008. Here is what is mentioned regarding Canada:

> *The income of the wealthiest has undergone a higher growth than their counterparts in other developed countries over the last ten years. According to the report, the average income of 10% of the richest Canadians is US$71,000, which is 30% above the OECD average (around US$54,000).*

The OECD believes the growing gap to be partly caused by the expense policies of the Canadian government. According to that organization, Canada's budgets allocated to families and employment are smaller than those of most OECD countries.[2]

Not so long ago, many experts were sceptical about the environmental analyses, claiming that the situation was not as dire as some people predicted. In the same vein, very few analysts predicted the extent of the food crisis facing us today, or the skyrocketing price of a barrel of oil.

---

1. United Nations Conference on Trade and Development, The Least Developed Countries Report, 2008.
2. OECD, "Income gap widens between Canada's rich and poor," *Canadian Press*, October 21st, 2008. Available on line at http://canadianpress.google.com/article/ALeqM5hpTxH6LhUx_paxYTA1q9R7ipHcrQ

Now everyone agrees that these problems exist without necessarily any agreement as to their causes, or the steps to be taken to deal with them. There is general agreement that population growth and rising consumption must be curtailed, but no consensus on the methods for achieving sustainable development. For instance, some experts advocate increasing agricultural production through the use of genetically modified seed, while others would prefer to see small-scale agriculture using, at the local level, less water and fewer chemicals. Ideas are numerous and increasingly founded on probative data. But when it comes to developing policies that could lead to action, the analyses are based on who will win and who will lose, and then corporate and government interests come into play.

The International Monetary Fund (IMF) and the World Bank have definitely failed at the task and must rethink their terms of aid to less developed countries. But it is encouraging to see that these organizations have now come to that realization. A major daily newspaper recently wrote that the IMF, "Long accused of having imposed a single economic development model on the countries under its wing... now states that every country is different and that the measures we advocate are also considerably different in nature."[3]

Are we going through a civilization crisis? That is what French political scientist, sociologist and essayist Emmanuel Todd posited in 1998, when he wrote:

> *The omnipotence of the economy is therefore nothing but an illusion. The drop in growth rates, the rise in inequality and poverty, the incoherence of monetary developments—all these are quite real events and they*

---

3. "*Le FMI sonne l'alarme*", *Le Devoir* (July 2, 2008): B1 (translation).

are economic in nature. But they only reflect and mask cultural and anthropological factors that run much deeper and are more distressing. [4]

The widening democratic gap our planet may be exposed to could create social ills and civil wars. As one of my history professors used to say, "when the populace is hungry, it takes to the streets." Indeed, it is not just the rhetoric of reformers that touched off history's major revolutions; quite often the stimulus was inflationary prices for food staples. Many authors have recently cited the 1976 Report by the Club of Rome, which predicted, without convincing many at that time, that well before we reach the physical limitations of the planet, serious social ills will appear because of the huge economic divide between rich and poor nations.[5]

Many political decisions have been based on fear. For example, increases in public health funding in the United States and Canada have occurred partly because of the avian flu crisis and the fear among the public of an outbreak of a world epidemic. Fear is also building because of the crises in the oil, food and environmental situations. I call that the panic button!

IS IT POSSIBLE TO HAVE AN APPROACH BASED UPON THE COMMON GOOD?

In the last few decades, many signals, including the AIDS epidemic, have reminded us that we are part of a globalized

---

4. Emmanuel Todd, *L'illusion économique, essai sur la stagnation des sociétés développées,* Paris, Gallimard, 1998, page 297. (translation)
5. Jan Tinbergen, Director, *Reshaping the International Order,* Dutton, New York, 1976, quoted by Haroldo Mattos de Lemos, "Saurons-nous réduire la consommation superflue?" in *Signons la paix avec la Terre* (English version: "Will we be able to reduce superfluous consumption?" in *Making Peace with the Earth*), Jérôme Bindé, dir., Paris, UNESCO, Albin Michel, 2007, p. 137.

society. A world pandemic is possible. However, if governments, entrepreneurs and citizens of developed countries plan to intervene in underprivileged societies and nations, the behaviour and cultures of those societies have to be taken into consideration.

As Lisa Sowle Cahill, the Christian theological ethicist, said: "The responsibility to support human life must now be placed in a global context."[6] Her suggestion is to move to a renewed vision of the common good.[7] I would add that our difficult problems have to be managed with creativity, innovation, and that a renewed vision of the global common good must be founded on social responsibility, justice, equity and solidarity. This is the price to pay to achieve the goal of sustainable development for future generations.

The richer countries need to change their ethics, values and the way they think about developing countries. Even as this agenda is difficult to pursue, it is becoming more understood and accepted by many members of the business community. Various communities have different reasons for adopting an agenda of change; however, a pragmatic consensus could emerge and lead to a short-term plan to resolve urgent problems. Still, a long-term agenda is also needed, one that would create a universal platform based on the respect of human dignity. Andrew Ferrier, CEO of the environmentally progressive New Zealand dairy co-operative Fonterra, has outlined how corporations can implement social and responsible standards and still make profits. However, Dennis Meadows, Director of the Institute for Policy and Social Science Research

---

6. *Bioethics and the Common Good*, Milwaukee, Marquette University Press, p. 76.
7. On that topic, interesting papers can be found in: Olivier Delas and Christian Deblock, *Le bien commun comme réponse politique à la mondialisation*, Brussels, Bruylant, 2003.

at the University of New Hampshire, has pointed out that culture, habits and behaviour are very difficult to change.

The June 2008 summit of the Food and Agriculture Organization of the United Nations (FAO), titled *World Food Security: The Challenges of Climate Change*, recently formulated a plan of action to fight hunger and poverty. This plan is based on a pledge from donor countries of approximately $6.5 billion. It had the support of Kofi Annan, former Secretary-General of the United Nations, Nobel Peace Prize Laureate and chair of The Alliance for a Green Revolution in Africa (AGRA). Yet, critics are saying that the summit is a total failure and that this proposal will contribute to the increase of world hunger and to the support of those who control 80% of agricultural commerce. Which avenue represents the truth?

It is clear that societies are facing many paradoxes and contradictions that oppose competitiveness and sustainable development. For example, the issue: "Too much focus on making energy cheaper could conflict with efforts to reduce consumption."[8]

In many fields of research and sectors of activity (environment, health, applied biotechnology) there is much questioning, and while the types of solutions proposed are not totally foreign to us, it is important to redefine them from a global standpoint.

In order to strike a balance between innovation, competitiveness and sustainable development, it is becoming increasingly apparent that globalization must be social as well as economic. We need to reinvent humanism, arriving at a new humanism that will integrate scientific advances, not only

---

8. "G8 Sees More Squalls on Horizon", *Financial Times* (June 12, 2008): 3.

to make life better for humanity today, but also for future generations.

What do we mean by "a global common-good approach?" We mean that we should move away from a nation-state focus to providing the least-developed countries with the capacity to nurture their own economies. It means that nations should not only care about their own well-being, but also about the international common good. That vision is the prerequisite for an innovative society that could be able to achieve sustainable development in the future as well as managing climate change, deforestation, water supply, pollution, and biodiversity erosion. The least-developed nations are asking not only for money, but also for help in increasing their capacity for research and technology. They need to develop know-how adapted to their own realities. They also need assistance in developing research infrastructure and governance models that take into account their culture and traditions. In this way, they will exercise sovereignty over their future.

Now that even developed countries are affected by globalization, the time has come to create a corpus of international instruments based on a vision of the common good. This implies that the public interest, which is the administrative manifestation of the common good, will inspire policy-makers in the development of national policies that include programs for the welfare of all human beings.

There are difficulties, but also great opportunities, in co-operating at the global level. We have seen that the multilateral organizations, UNESCO included, are ready to work with other international organizations like the World Health Organization (WHO), the International Monetary Fund (IMF), the World Bank and the Organisation for Economic Co-operation and Development (OECD). Together, they have the capacity to create development policies based upon a plan to manage natural resources, food supply, and energy and technology that will establish an equilibrium between growth and sustainable development. Over the last decades, these organizations have often worked alone in defining their agendas only with their members. What is needed now is more solidarity and a rapprochement between humanitarian and economic organizations with social and economic agendas. In this way we can maximize the benefits of globalization and minimize its negative effects.

Too much rampant capitalism—capitalism that does not care about human resources but only about making a profit—pervades and creates havoc in many countries. This has to change and there is a movement, although too slow, in that direction. More large corporations are getting involved in programs based on equity, solidarity and responsibility. However, best-selling author Henry Mintzberg said, referring to Nobel Laureate and economist Milton Friedman and the Chicago School: "*The Business of Business is Business* and corporations do not have to be preoccupied with the social agenda which is the business of the State." Mintzberg is of the view that the economic interests of corporations often have disastrous social consequences. They do not have to pay for the human and social impacts of their decisions as long as they are not breaking the law. Mintzberg admires corporations that are willing to do good because he believes they must not forget that society belongs to citizens and communities. [9]

---

9. These ideas were developed in an interview. Jacinthe Tremblay, "Mintzberg sur : La responsabilité sociale. Entre la bonne volonté et le marketing", *La Presse*, (December 22, 2007): business section, page 7.

Populations across the world need to be involved in the building of their futures. The capacity to innovate and anticipate strategic change comes with both formal and informal education, good governance, and with public participation in the decision-making process.

To economist Ricardo Petrella, the common good revolves around equal access to food, shelter, energy, education, health, etc. He writes that it is urgent to: "put the economy to work for the *global common good*."[10] Such an agenda may seem utopian, but it would definitely be innovative! Whether out of fear of the impacts that our current methods will have or for more noble reasons, let us hope it will lead to a productive synergy that will drive competition to develop a world agenda that includes an economy and society that complement each other. As Max Weber, the German sociologist and economist also said,

> *Certainly all historical experience confirms—that man would not have achieved the possible unless time and again he had reached out for the impossible.*[11]

At present, in our knowledge-based societies, we have the technological capability to deal with many challenges. It would be wise for us to put that capability to work in the interest of the common good and develop new models for living together. The model proposed in a recent publication could be represented as follows: [12]

---

10. *Le bien commun*, Brussells, Labor, 1996, page 9. (translation)
11. *Le savant et le politique*, Paris, Plon, 10/18, 1963, page 221. (translation)
12. See: Michèle S. Jean and Béatrice Godard, "Santé éthique et bien commun : que voulons-nous dire?" in: Bartha Maria Knoppers and Yann Joly, Eds, *La santé et le bien commun*, Montréal, Thémis, 2008, pages 121-137.

This concept of the common good should also be integrated in a positive international legal framework. That is a major challenge but, as international law expert Jacques-Yvan Morin wrote:

> *Humanizing globalization is an ambitious scheme. Legal scholars cannot succeed in this task, however, unless they themselves believe in the existence and requirements of a common heritage for all nations. Today, the only valid "realism" consists of globalizing the common good as efficiently and quickly as possible... Let us be bold enough to declare that globalization can apply to the common good just as well as the problems it purports to help solve.[13]*

13. "L'éthique, le bien commun et la mondialisation", 3rd lecture series of the *Canada Research Chair in Law and Medicine*, September 20, 2006, Faculty of Law, Université de Montréal, http://hdl.handle.net/1866/749 (TRANSLATION).

BIOGRAPHICAL NOTES

JÉRÔME BINDÉ

Director of the Division of Foresight at UNESCO

Deputy Assistant Director-General for Social and Human Sciences and Director of the Division of Foresight at UNESCO. Secretary-General of the Council of the Future, Founding Member of the Academy of Latinity, Member of the Club of Rome and of the World Academy of Art and Science. Coordinator of the *21ˢᵗ Century Talks* and the *21ˢᵗ Century Dialogues*, and editor of the two anthologies of the series of encounters: *Keys to the 21ˢᵗ Century* and *The Future of Values*. Director of the UNESCO World Report *Towards Knowledge Societies*.

Principal co-author, with Federico Mayor, and coordinator of the forward-looking UNESCO world report, *The World Ahead: Our Future in the Making*.

Dr. Paul Cappon

President and CEO
Canadian Council on Learning (CCL)

Dr. Paul Cappon was named President and Chief Executive Officer of the Canadian Council on Learning in October 2004. A prominent educator, doctor and administrator, Dr. Cappon has been a life-long education advocate, community supporter and author of numerous publications on learning and community medicine.

He has earned degrees in several fields, including a Ph.D. in sociology from the Université de Paris, a medical degree (M.D.) from McMaster and a family medicine specialization from Dalhousie.

Since the 1970s, Dr. Cappon has built a remarkable public service career. He has been a faculty member at several Canadian universities including Laurentian, McGill, Saint Mary's and UBC, teaching both sociology and medicine.

Most recently, he served as the Director General of the Council of Ministers of Education, Canada.

In addition to his contributions in academia, Dr. Cappon served, among other roles, as Director of AIDS studies at the Montreal General Hospital. Dr. Cappon is a member of the International Coordinating Council at the State of the World Forum, as well as being a member of the Historica Council of the Historica Foundation of Canada. He is also Chair of the Policy Action Group on Learning for the Commission on Globalization.

In 2002, Dr. Cappon received the Commemorative Queen Elizabeth II Golden Jubilee Medal for his significant contribution to his profession.

He is fluent in French and English and has a working knowledge of Italian and German.

ANDREW FERRIER
Chief Executive Officer
Fonterra

Andrew Ferrier has been Chief Executive Officer of Fonterra Co-operative Group since September 2003, bringing with him a background of generating stronger performances from companies in both the consumer products sector and the commodities market. He has more than 22 years of experience at the senior executive level, with 14 years as a Chief Executive in operating and holding companies. In his career he has dealt continuously with both free trade environments and heavily regulated environments, experiences now being applied at Fonterra.

Mr. Ferrier is founding Chairman of Global Dairy Platform, an international organization whose mission is to provide insight and guidance in the promotion of the healthy consumption of dairy products. He also sits on the Growth and Innovation Advisory Board (GIAB), which provides high-level, independent strategic advice to the New Zealand government on growth and innovation issues.

Mr. Ferrier has a Bachelor of Business Administration from the University of New Brunswick and a Master of Business Administration from Concordia University, both in Canada.

ANGEL GURRÍA

Secretary-General
Organisation for Economic Co-operation & Development (OECD)

Angel Gurría came to the Organisation for Economic Co-operation & Development (OECD) following a distinguished career in public service, including two ministerial posts in his native country of Mexico.

As Mexico's Minister of Foreign Affairs (1994-1998) Mr. Gurría promoted the ideas of dialogue and consensus-building in his approach to global issues. As Minister of Finance and Public Credit (1998-2000) he smoothly steered Mexico's economy through a change of administration.

As Secretary-General since June 2006, Mr. Gurría has reinforced the OECD's role as a centre for global dialogue and debate on economic policy issues. He also has effected internal modernization and reform.

Under Mr. Gurría's leadership, the OECD has agreed to open membership talks with Chile, Estonia, Israel, Russia and Slovenia and to strengthen links with other major emerging economies, including Brazil, China, India, Indonesia and South Africa, with a view to possible membership.

Mr. Gurría also works with the Population Council in New York and the Center for Global Development based in Washington. He chaired the International Task Force on Financing Water for All and continues to be deeply involved in water issues. He is a member of the International Advisory Board of Governors of the Centre for International Governance Innovation in Canada, and was the first recipient of the Globalist of the Year Award of the Canadian International Council.

Mr. Gurría holds a B.A. in Economics from UNAM (Mexico) and an M.A. in Economics from Leeds University (United Kingdom). He speaks Spanish, French, English, Portuguese, Italian and some German.

Donald Kaberuka

President
African Development Bank Group (AfDB)

As President of the Bank Group, Donald Kaberuka chairs the Boards of the African Development Bank and the African Development Fund, the soft loan arm of the Group.

Mr. Kaberuka was educated in Tanzania and the United Kingdom where he obtained his M. Phil. (Econ.) and a Ph.D. in Economics from Glasgow University in Scotland.

He served as Rwanda's Minister of Finance and Economic Planning from 1997 to 2005, and has been widely acknowledged as the principal architect of the successful post-war reconstruction and economic reform program in that country. He initiated and implemented major economic and governance reforms in the fiscal, monetary, budgetary and structural domains including independence of the Central Banks. These reforms resulted in the widely acclaimed recovery of the Rwandan economy and sustained economic growth which enabled the country to benefit from debt cancellations under the Highly Indebted Poor Countries (HIPC) Initiative in April 2005.

Mr. Kaberuka had over 12 years' experience in the Banking industry, trade, finance, international commodity business and development issues, before he joined the government.

As minister of Finance and Economic Planning, the new AfDB President was Governor for Rwanda at the World Bank, the International Monetary Fund (IMF) and the African Development Bank.

He is fluent in English, French and Swahili.

JEAN LEMIERRE

Former President of the European Bank for Reconstruction and
Development (EBRD)

Jean Lemierre, born in June 1950, has had a long
and distinguished career in international finance. As
Director of the French Treasury from 1995, he served
as a member of the European Monetary Committee
from 1995 to 1998, and prior to taking up his position
at the EBRD was Chairman of the European
Economic and Financial Committee and Chairman
of the Paris Club. Previously he had served as Head
of France's Internal Revenue Service, Head of the Tax
Policy Administration and as Head of the Private
Office of the Minister of Economy and Finance.

Mr. Lemierre is a graduate of the Institut d'Études
politiques de Paris (Economy). He graduated from
the École nationale d'administration (ÉNA).

DENNIS MEADOWS, PH.D.

President of the Laboratory for Interactive Learning and Professor
Emeritus for Systems Policy of the University of New Hampshire.

Dennis Meadows is a systems analyst and environmental educator. He was an institute director for 35 years and held tenured positions at three different universities in business, engineering and the social sciences.

His 10 books have been translated into more than 30 languages. One was awarded the German Peace Prize in the 1970s and it was selected to be among the 10 most important environmental texts of the 20th century.

His most recent book, *Limits to Growth — the 30-Year Update*, was judged to be the most important book on the future published in German in 2006.

He designs sophisticated management-training simulations on issues related to the environment and sustainable development. Corporations, universities and other institutions use them in training programs around the world.

Mr. Meadows has served on the management boards of companies in Europe and the United States. The firms are active in renewable energy, software development and social health insurance.

He has lived and worked in six countries; he has lectured or consulted to corporate and government groups in more than 40 nations.

Mr. Meadows has won many honours, prizes and awards. They include the 1975 prize of the Association for Nature Protection in Bavaria; a 1989 Fulbright Fellowship to the Soviet Union; the 2005 prize for Environmental Communication of EURONATUR; and the 2006 Presidential Order of Honour of the Hungarian Republic; the Medium Cross, and the 2007 Peace Clock of the German Committee for UNESCO.

He has honorary doctorates from three European universities for his contributions to environmental education.

THE HONOURABLE MADELEINE MEILLEUR

Minister of Community and Social Services and Minister
Responsible for Francophone Affairs of Ontario

On October 30, 2007, the Honourable Dalton McGuinty re-appointed Madeleine Meilleur as Minister of Community and Social Services. She also remains Minister Responsible for Francophone Affairs.

As Minister of Community and Social Services, Minister Meilleur plays an active role in putting forward her leadership abilities to ensure that the Ministry offers help to the people who need it most.

As Minister of Culture, Minister Meilleur spearheaded efforts to introduce a new and strengthened Ontario Heritage Act, concluding 30 years of efforts to provide better heritage protection. The new act received Royal Assent in April 2005, which brought Ontario in line with leading jurisdictions in heritage conservation.

A leader committed to building bridges between linguistic communities, Minister Meilleur established, as Minister Responsible for Francophone Affairs, the Provincial Advisory Committee on Francophone Affairs.

A registered nurse and lawyer specializing in labour and employment law, Minister Meilleur brought leadership to numerous committees and task forces. Minister Meilleur was elected to the provincial legislature in 2003 after more than a decade in municipal politics. From 1991 to 2003, she represented the City of Vanier and the Regional Municipality of Ottawa-Carleton and served as a councillor in the new City of Ottawa.

GÉRARD MESTRALLET
Chairman and CEO of GDF SUEZ

Before his election as Chairman and CEO of GDF SUEZ, Gérard Mestrallet had been Chairman and CEO of Suez (2001-2008).

Gérard Mestrallet is Chairman of the Board of Directors of SUEZ Énergie Services, Suez Environment, Houlival, SUEZ-Tractebel (Belgium). He is Chairman of Hisusa (Spain). He is also Vice-President of the Board of Directors of Electrabel and Vice-Chairman of Aguas de Barcelona (Spain). He is a Member of the Board of Trustees of AXA, Chairman of the Paris EUROPLACE Association and Member of the Council of the French Institute of Directors. He is also Director of Saint-Gobain (France), Pargesa Holding SA (Switzerland).

Gérard Mestrallet is a graduate of the École polytechnique and the École nationale d'administration (ÉNA), in Paris.

CHRISTINE OCKRENT

Writer and journalist

Executive Director, Société de l'audiovisuel extérieur de la France

Christine Ockrent is Director General of France's Société de l'audiovisuel extérieur.

She is also on the board of directors of the Metro International press group and writes for a number of French-language newspapers.

Ms. Ockrent is a former editor of the weekly journal *L'Express* and *L'Européen* magazine.

The first woman to anchor the 8 o'clock news on French television, Ms. Ockrent has produced and hosted a number of debates and feature reports, for which she has received various French and international distinctions.

She began her career as a journalist with American television broadcasters NBC News and CBS News, and worked for eight years on CBS's newsmagazine *60 Minutes*.

Ms. Ockrent has authored thirteen books, and serves on the boards of l'Institut Français de Relations Internationales (IFRI), the European Council on Foreign Relations (ECFR), the International Crisis Group, the Center for European Reform, Human Rights Watch France, Reporters Sans Frontières and the Women's Forum for the Economy and Society.

A graduate of l'Institut d'Études Politiques de Paris, Ms. Ockrent is an Officer of the Légion d'honneur, an Officer of the Ordre du Mérite and an Officer of the Ordre de Léopold.

GIL RÉMILLARD

Founding Chairman, International Economic Forum of the
Americas / Conference of Montreal
Professor, École nationale d'administration publique (ÉNAP)
Counsel, Fraser Milner Casgrain LLP

Gil Rémillard holds degrees in philosophy and political science and a Ph.D in law, and has practised in the field of education, politics and private legal practice.

As Minister of Justice for more than five years, Mr. Rémillard presided over the reform of the *Civil Code of Québec*, implemented on January 1st of 1994. Since 1994, Mr. Rémillard has been a professor at the École nationale d'administration publique du Québec (ÉNAP), and counsel for the law firm of Fraser Milner Casgrain LLP. He is also chairman of the Institute of International Studies in Administration of Montréal and chairman and founder of the International Economic Forum of the Americas/Conference of Montreal, as well as president and publisher of the economic magazine *FORCES*.

In September 2008, he was appointed Chairman of the Board of Directors of the Université de Sherbrooke.

He has published several works and papers, of which *Le fédéralisme canadien Tome I et II*. Doctor Honoris Causa of the Faculty of Law, Economics and Science of the Université d'Aix-Marseille, he was awarded, in 1994, the *Médaille du Mérite du Barreau du Québec*, and in 2001, he received the Order of Canada. In 2004, he received the *Ordre national du Québec* and was honoured as Knight of *l'Ordre de la Légion d'honneur* by the President of the French Republic.

LUCIE SAUVÉ

Holder of the Canada Research Chair in Environmental Education
Université du Québec à Montréal (UQAM)

Lucie Sauvé is a full professor at the Université du Québec à Montréal (UQAM) Faculty of Education and Pedagogy. She is also holder of the Canada Research Chair in Environmental Education, and a member of UQAM's Institut des Sciences de l'environnement and Institut Santé et Société.

She is a research associate with DIALOG, a Québec network for the discussion of aboriginal issues, a director of the international journal *Éducation relative à l'environnement — Regards, Recherche, Réflexions* and director of the Scientific Committee of the Réseau International Francophone de Recherche en Éducation Relative à l'Environnement (RefERE).

She is also in charge of UQAM's short graduate study program in environmental education. Prof. Sauvé's main areas of specialization are environmental health education (particularly food sovereignty and security), scientific education, ecodevelopmental education, the challenges of teaching educators (including distance education) and grassroots environmental participation.

For the last 15 years, Prof. Sauvé has directed major international cooperation projects in Latin America, including "Écodéveloppement Communautaire et Santé Environnementale en Bolivie," a project designed to support Bolivian Amazon partner universities in their education, research and social development efforts dealing with socio-ecological equity, particularly food and water.

Rosalía Arteaga Serrano

President of the Foundation for the Integration and Development
of Latin America (FIDAL)

Rosalía Arteaga is the former President and Vice-President of the Republic of Ecuador.

She has also served her country as Minister of Education, Culture and Sports. She is active throughout Latin America and around the world in issues of the environment, education, culture, heritage and the advancement of women. She has addressed many international conferences on the environment including "Natural Resources: A Shared Responsibility" in Vienna (2007) and the "Congress of Biodiversity" in Rome (2008).

Ms. Arteaga has held prestigious posts with many influential international organizations. These include: the Editorial Board of the Encyclopaedia Britannica, General Secretary of the Amazon Cooperation Treaty Organization, President of the Organization for Preinversion of Latin America and the Caribbean, Vice-President of the International Federation of Women Lawyers, High Commissioner of the Network of Regional Universities of Latin America, Member of the Culture Foundation of Ecuador and a member of the Board of the Agronomic Tropical Center of Investigation and Education.

In the media, Ms. Arteaga also contributes to the daily newspaper La Hora in Quito and Ecuador News: New York. She writes for and is a Director of the Educational Edu@news magazine and the ecological magazine Verd (Green). She produces television's "Face to Face" with Rosalía. Her published works also include the following books: *Hours*, *Gente* (People), *Cinco Poemas* (Five Poems) and *Jerónimo*.

In academia, Ms. Arteaga is also a Professor at Gabriel Renè Moreno University in Santa Cruz de la Sierra in Bolivia. She has received a Doctor of Law degree from the University of Cuenca (Ecuador), and

also attended the Journalism School at the Catholic
University of Cuenca. She holds a Masters in Basic
Education and Rescue of Cultural Values in Latin
America, from the Federal university of Bahía, Brazil.

Michèle S. Jean

President, Canadian Commission for UNESCO

Michèle S. Jean was born in Québec City. She has a master's degree in history, a master's degree in andragogy and an honorary doctorate in law.

She pursued a long career in the provincial and federal civil service, first as Canada's Deputy Minister of Health from 1993 to 1998, and as Special Advisor to Canada's Minister of Foreign Affairs (Health and Social Affairs) assigned to the Permanent Mission of Canada to the European Union in Brussels from 1998 to 2000.

She is currently a visiting scholar at the Université de Montréal's Public Law Research Centre, Faculty of Law, and a doctorand in applied social studies, bioethics option.

She was president of UNESCO's International Bioethics Committee from 2002 to 2005, at which time the Committee drafted the Universal Declaration on Bioethics and Human Rights, which was adopted at the UNESCO General Conference in October 2005.

She has been President of the Canadian Commission for UNESCO since 2006, and President of the FRSQ's research ethics and scientific integrity board since 2008. Her research deals with bioethics and the common good from a universal perspective.

Ms. Jean is co-author of *L'Histoire des femmes au Québec depuis quatre siècles* (1992). She was selected by the American Biographical Institute as one of the Great Women of the 21st Century.